The Message of Love:
Understanding Sin and the Law

The Message of Love:
Understanding Sin and the Law

by:
Oddeth S. Burton

Editors:
Pedro A. Hall
Beverlie Ramocan-Woodland

iUniverse, Inc.
Bloomington

The Message of Love: Understanding Sin and the Law

iUniverse books may be ordered through booksellers or by contacting:

iUniverse
1663 Liberty Drive
Bloomington, IN 47403
www.iuniverse.com
1-800-Authors (1-800-288-4677)

ISBN: 978-1-4620-5245-5 (sc)
ISBN: 978-1-4620-5246-2 (ebk)

Printed in the United States of America

iUniverse rev. date: 11/28/2011

CONTENTS

Preface

The Message of Love was inspired by the Holy Spirit of God and the encouragement of friends who thought that this inspiration should be written and shared with others. I became annoyed at the monotonous way in which the church presents its doctrines using so many other materials other than the Word of God, the Bible. Chief among these doctrines is the issue of God's love for mankind and how it is expressed. Many times only the New Testament is used to explain such love but this really cannot be properly done without starting starting from the beginning-the Genesis story. Any defence for truth must begin at the beginning and hence the inspiration to examine the love of God by exploring the issue of law and sin. Once there is an understanding of what happened in the Garden of Eden the rest becomes easy.

This book is a culmination of two years of research and shows what sin is and sin's solution due to the love of God through the person of Jesus Christ. I would like to thank those who provided me with books, offered prayers and encouragement and even edited a line or two. May God bless you all.

Introduction

Salvation speaks to the love of God for humanity and is a matter of life and death. Interestingly, many publications are done in an attempt to explain man's salvation, especially as it relates to Sin and its relationship to the Law. This topic of the Law is fervently debated in theological circles and is more of an academic and philosophical contest than a matter of revealed truth from the throne of God. The debaters, whose arguments are said to be more convincing, are the ones most likely to be believed; even if the premise on which the conclusion is drawn is faulty. However, coming close to what seems like the truth is not enough—it is not the truth. The Jamaican adage "nearly neva (never) kill a bird" means "almost doesn't count". No matter how close one gets to the truth, if it's not the truth, it's just not the truth. It is accepting the revealed Word of God through the guidance and direction of God's Holy Spirit as truth that matters. It is the Spirit of God through His Holy Word—the Bible, that sets the tone for the use of the terms 'sin' and 'law,' negating all other scholarly material. The Bible interprets itself. It is the road map of the Kingdom of God. The truth of God is not a "belief contest" that needs to be defended by those who have the intellectual prowess to do so. There is no defence against the truth. The truth sets one free from the use of senseless chatter over words that ask the question—Is salvation about man or God or both?

There is a need for a balanced understanding on the Gospel message as it relates to the subject of sin and the law. This is not a trifling matter as the world is enslaved unto death and is called to repentance from law breaking which sin brought about. If man is called to repentance, what Law breaking is man repenting of? What did man 'turn away from' or 'lost out on' that required the blood of Jesus Christ to atone for him? What does this process of reconciliation demand for man's salvation? When these and other questions are answered, the big picture of the purpose of God and mankind will take centre stage. It has been said that the most effective method for training authorities to identify counterfeit money is to have them study what real money looks and feels like. If we are to know what the law and sin are we will have to look at the real issue of sin. The apostle Peter said in first Peter 3:15, "and *be* ready always to *give* an answer to every man that asks you a reason of the hope that is in you with meekness and fear."

The Bible teaches that Christ loves us and died for our sins and that His shed blood cleanses us and sets us free from the bondage of sin. It also teaches about the freedom that grace gives by keeping God's Law. But how is this grace meted out? Is it in hiding the true definition of sin? If sin is lawlessness and the assumption is made that the Law is the Ten Commandments, what law did Adam and Eve transgress to put the entire human race under such curse? Did the second Adam in the person of Christ do away with or fulfil the law? What was the symbolic significance of the fruit Adam and Eve ate? Was it a literal fruit or sex, as some have asserted? If not what was it?

The Bible again teaches that Christ did not do away with the Law. Christ revealed in Matthew 5:17-19 that He did not come to do away with the Law but to fulfil it. If this is so, how did He fulfil it? If Christ fulfilled the law, there must be a definitive and clear path given in the scripture through the guidance of God's Holy Spirit as to how it was fulfilled. If no such path is given, then it would appear that Christendom has no sure foundation but has built its house on sinking sand. If the foundation is shaky, then they ought to be listening to the cries of atheism, that the possibility of God not existing might be true.

The fact that religious leaders are in academic mystification about the Law, speaks to their understanding of the word of God. This may be due to the fact that many preach universal salvation without the universal acceptance of the Law. The Law is deemed as obsolete, a yoke of bondage, a grievous burden, a remorseless enemy and, therefore, holds no significance except for its morality; which is relative based on culture and tradition (i.e. to take the view that the law was meant for Israel only).

Could it be that the search for answers is in the wrong places and sources or that the right source was sought (John 5:39) but a falling short occurred because of self—righteousness? Has The Church of God, (not an organization but an organised body of believers whose belief is centred on truth) that Christ established, been fulfilling its mandate or has it joined the numerous churches/organizations existing in the name of God and Christianity, in mere "wrangling over words aimed at causing confusion?" (2 Timothy 2:14). If God is about truth and love, can these be limited to an organization or nation marketed for sale by the best in marketing and sales to fill churches? Or, do the truth and love of God speak to the "call" upon the lives of individuals to live righteously through the Spirit of God, which created them? Whatever the case may be, those to whom the truth has been revealed have an obligation to God and the human race to teach it and answer the questions that will lead to the redemption of their neighbours' soul and to those that may come under their influence.

Humanity is in dire need of answers, and Christ in Matthew 9:37 said to His disciples, *"the harvest truly is plentiful, but the labourers are few."* Only a few disciples can teach and preach the message of love that Christ taught and left for His followers to do. May God open the reader's mind to the understanding of this great and awesome plan of salvation through this medium.

Let's get started!

Sin and the Law

The topic of sin and the Law is one of the most tedious of tasks ever undertaken in religious circles and so contrary are the views that it leaves no room for doubt that people do not know what sin and the Law are. A Law does not exist in a vacuum. It exists because it operates within certain parameters of universality and immutability, enforced by a government. Yet, some have made the law to be a debatable subject matter of moral codes found within the codified Ten Commandments (minus the fourth) given to Israel by God through Moses and the "grace and truth' that came through Jesus Christ (John 1:17). They fail to acknowledge that prior to the codified Law given to the nation of Israel, the universality of the law existed (Romans 5:12-14) along with its consequences and that it was 'human sinfulness *that* made it necessary for God's will to be communicated in written form'.[1] Sin entered humanity because the law was broken by one man and not a nation. If we accept the argument that the Law was only given to a particular set of people (Jews) excluding all others (Gentiles) we will have to accept that the universality of sin and redemption does not apply to all but to the Jews only. One will have to conclude that the saving grace of God which the Bible teaches in

---

[1]   Bahnsen. Greg L. (1996) In the book *Five Views on Law and Gospel.* Zondervan Publishing House. Grand Rapids, Michigan. (60)

John 3:16, does not apply to all peoples hence cannot be the guiding principle for man's salvation. That is, only the nation to which the law was given, salvation is offered. It leaves the majority of mankind in the same position he was at the beginning, after the first act—"having no hope and without God in the world" (Ephesians 2:12). If salvation is offered to all of humanity, the law applies to all of humanity. Salvation is universal and, therefore, what the law speaks, it speaks that "the whole world [may be] held accountable *to the giver of the Law* (Rom. 3:19)"[2]—God.

In 1 John 3:4, sin is defined as the transgression of the Law, or lawlessness, "a deliberate and rebellious violation of God's will"[3]. This text is the only direct definition of sin given in the Bible. Note carefully, that this definition was posited many years after Christ's death and with the knowledge of the Old Testament. Therefore, sin cannot be defined without the law; for it is the law that defines/dictates what sin is. Paul wrote in Romans 7:7-8, "what shall we say then? Is the law sin? Certainly not! On the contrary I would not have known sin except through the law. For I would not have known covetousness unless the law had said, "you shall not covet." But sin, taking opportunity by the commandment, produced in me all manner of evil desire.' What law is Paul speaking about? Was it the law of the Ten Commandments or the tenth commandment? The text further goes on to say that "for apart from the law sin was dead", meaning that if there is no Law, there can be no sin. Sin cannot exist if there is no Law. Thomas Schreiner notes

---

[2]   ibid 110

[3]   Schreiner. Thomas R. (2003) *Romans.* Baker Book House. Grand Rapids, Michigan.

that "the law actually becomes an abettor to sin, and sin as an alien power, employs the law to accomplish its own ends,"[4] thus sin is necessary to the fulfilling of the Law. Sounds contradictory? It is not! Romans 3:20 confirms this noting that *'for by the law is the knowledge of sin'*. The knowledge of sin came through the law. Therefore, sin and the law are inseparable entities in the great plan of the God. Romans 5:13-14 states, "for until the law sin was in the world . . . nevertheless death reigned from Adam to Moses, even over those who had not sinned according to the likeness of the transgression of Adam . . ." What was the sin that was in the world before the law and reigned from Adam to Moses and the succeeding generations?

But what is this sin? Is it the breaking of the Ten Commandments in an outward physical manner or is there more? Scriptures reveal where Christ amplified the law in the New Testament to show its spiritual intent. It also divulges that Satan and the angelic host broke the Law before mankind did. However, it was the act (or lack thereof) of the first Adam that required the life of the second Adam to redeem mankind. How did the act of the first Adam differ from that of Jesus Christ, the second Adam? All this is enveloped in the plan of salvation which was before the foundation of the world (1 Peter 1: 20; Revelation 13:8) and, therefore, must have included sin. As a result, SIN, through the existence of the Law, has a beginning and we are assured by God, through Christ who kept the Law, that it will have an end. (Revelation 20:14-15)

---

[4]   Ibid 359

All have sinned (by breaking the law), Romans 3:23. Therefore, for anyone to understand sin and its relationship to the Law, he/she must start at the beginning, and since all things began with God and ultimately will end with Him (Genesis 1:1; Revelation 1:8; 21:6), let's start there. The nature of sin cannot be fully understood if one does not know the truth about what it is, the root of its existence and how it came to be associated with the breaking of the law and also God's purpose for its existence.

There are various terms within the English language that are used to define Law. However, these like the Hebrew and Greek terms, give a very narrow understanding of the Biblical term. One must keep in mind that the word "law" is used interchangeably in scriptures and is dependent upon the context for proper interpretation and understanding. There are basically three references in scripture relating to the law. These are "Law of God", "Law of Moses" and the "Law of Christ". The "Law of God expresses the mind of the *Creator*, and is binding upon all rational creatures".[5] It is God's unchangeable standard and was impressed upon man from the beginning. "The Law of Moses is the entire system of legislation, judicial and ceremonial *requirements* which Jehovah gave to Israel during the time they were in the wilderness."[6] An example of the Law of God and the Law of Moses is found in Nehemiah 8:1 where the term "Law of Moses" is mentioned but at the same time referred to as "Law of God" in verses 8 and 18 of the same text. Finally,

---

[5] Pink, A. W. 1999. *The Law and the Saint*. Logos Research Systems, Inc.: Oak Harbor, WA

[6] Pink, A. W. 1999. *The Law and the Saint*. Logos Research Systems, Inc.: Oak Harbor, WA

The "Law of Christ" is God's . . . Law, but in the hands of the Mediator. It is the Law which Christ Himself was "made under" (Gal. 4:4). It is the Law which was "in His heart" (Psa. 40:8). It is the Law which He came to "fulfill" (Matt. 5:17). The "Law of God" is now termed "the Law of Christ" as it relates to *Christians.*"[7]

It is to be noted that Moses never wrote a single law and that all the laws of Moses were given by God hence they are the laws of God and Christ. Therefore, when the law is spoken of, it is speaking to the will and commands of God.

Then again, the issue is not about the wrangling over words to create more confusion (2 Timothy 2:14). It is aimed at spiritually motivating the reader to seek God through His Spirit and the reading of His Word and to live according to the law that is geared at saving humanity from destroying itself. These truths are firmly established in His Word thus revealing what sin and the Law is.

The Law in its fullest, most complete sense, according to Romans 7:14, ". . . is spiritual," because the Law cannot be separated from its giver, who is by nature Spirit (John 4:24) and is God. The Lawgiver's plan was to bring order to creation through His Spirit. Genesis 1:1-2 reads, *"In the beginning God created the heavens and the earth. The earth was without form, and void; and darkness was on the face of the deep. And the Spirit of God was hovering over the face of the waters."* God, through His Spirit and by His very being, ordered the refashioning (Psalm 104:30) of the

---

[7]   ibid

earth to operate by Law. This "Spirit of God" is the very essence by which the law operates; in that the law functions by Spirit—God's Holy Spirit. It is not a third person of a triune God as currently taught by some. Notice that God didn't just speak, He acted; "the Spirit of God moved,"—it is active. "'God in Genesis 1; is One who acts and speaks." His reality is seen in his acts; he is not an entity who can be conceived of apart from his works."[8] Also of note is that God did not just establish himself as Spirit but one with an image and likeness given to man (Genesis 1:26-28)—a person with a body and mind. This God created/brought forth the invisible (Hebrews 11:3) by the word of His mouth for a particular reason that has been confirmed as His love for humanity. Love is something that must be expressed. This was revealed by God creating mankind in His own image and likeness and later by the offering of His Son Jesus Christ at Calvary. Mankind is the reason the world exists; man is not "as an imitation of the divine image but to *be* the divine image".[9] God loves mankind as He loves himself. Thus, His command to 'love thy neighbour as thyself' (Matthew 5:43; 22:39; Romans 13:9; Galatians 5:14) and through this love deemed the world inhabitable for man because He sees himself in man. Therefore, God is love (1 John 4: 8, 16). Love is the totality of whom God and the law determine. Love is faith in action; the law by definition (James 2:8-24).

God, being Spirit and also a reproducing family of beings can only reproduce by Spirit—The Law through

---

8   Wenham, G. J. 2002. *Vol. 1: Word Biblical Commentary: Genesis 1-15*. Word Biblical Commentary. Word, Incorporated: Dallas
9   ibid

which He exists. Note the use of "*us*" in Genesis 1:26. This shows a consultation and covenant (Titus 1:2; Acts 2:23) between the members of the family of reproducing Beings. Some have suggested that God was addressing angels, but scripture reveals that angels were not made in the image and likeness of God (Hebrews 2:5-9; Psalm 8:5). The word for 'God' in Hebrew is Elohim and is plural in form, meaning more than one and is not limited to a particular number. Further, the New Testament's acceptance of Jesus Christ as God would become void. He must have been addressing His equal. Presently, they exist as two distinct personalities and are the only species of Beings of their kind existing. We further see the oneness of the Godhead being demonstrated in the incarnated Word (John 1:14). One was the WORD, who was God incarnate in the person of Jesus Christ. The other was God who later became the Father of the WORD through the same Spirit. Deuteronomy 6:4 reads, '*Hear, O Israel: The LORD our God, the LORD is one!*' One in essence, power, purpose and being; not the Unitarian dogma promoted by some. As reproducing Beings, their aim is to create more beings after their kind—the God kind through the salvation process of conception and reproduction. This reproduction is called character, which helps us in understanding the creation of mankind in their "image and likeness". If man is in the image of God, then the "the image of God must characterize man's whole being, not simply his mind . . . , on the one hand, or his body, on the other."[10] Seeing that sin is the transgression of the law, character reproduction must be seen as operating

---

[10] Wenham, G. J. 2002. *Vol. 1: Word Biblical Commentary: Genesis 1-15*. Word Biblical Commentary . Word, Incorporated: Dallas

by obedience to a particular set of laws. Character is the ability to bear fruit (of good or evil), which can only be produced through obedience to the spirit of that particular Law. Mankind exercising the choice given to him of his own freewill develops it over time. Man is of the dust and physical but will transcend to the spiritual (that of being born into the Kingdom of God) through obedience to the Law. Oswald Chambers states,

> "We have to remember that God created Adam a "son of God," and God required Adam to develop himself by obeying Him; that obedience necessarily involved the sacrifice of the natural life to transform it into spiritual life, and this was to be done by a series of . . . choices."[11]

God formed man from the dust of the earth by the Law of His Spirit so that man might become "God" by that very same Law. This is the message of the Gospel of the Eternal Kingdom of God. That is, man's destiny and redemption is to become God; as God is God. God is Spirit and will transform His created beings fully into His image and likeness (Philippians 3:21). That's the codified message of the Gospel and of the Ten Commandments—God first, then man.

Now let's examine how the transgression of the Law occurred and God's continued purpose for including man.

---

[11]   Chambers, O. 1996, c1960. *The Philosophy of Sin: And other studies on the problem of man's moral life*. Marshall, Morgan & Scott: Hants UK

Sin in the Angelic Realm

God created angels in the heavens (Colossians 1:16; Nehemiah 9:6) along with Lucifer the anointed cherub, being perfect in all his ways (Ezekiel 28:15), but not possessing the immortality of God. Lucifer, who became Satan, is described as the "supernatural originator of sin who stands next to God in power."[12] Angels are spirit beings whose character development was not different from that of mankind. God did not create angels as robots to be used at His whim and fancy, but made them with the ability to think and choose their own destiny based upon knowledge and free will. This freedom gave Lucifer (who was the brightest and most loved of all the beings, until iniquity was found in him Ezekiel 28:15) and others with him, the opportunity to rebel against his Creator. Notice Satan's sin was not termed a transgression but rebellion. Sin only became a transgression of the commandment after Adam's experience in the Garden. In order to reproduce character, there must be tests of obedience given to ascertain one's temperament and credibility. It is not shaped by opportunities for self enhancement but by rightly learning to respond to the will of the Creator. Once character has been formed over the period of time for testing, one's character is sealed for eternity. Angels do not possess the divine spiritual character of God; that is His love—the spiritual mind of God. They are ministering spirits (Hebrews 1:14) created to abet human beings in the marvellous plan of salvation. They are not to be worshipped (Colossians 2:18) or prayed to.

---

[12] Chambers, O. 1996, c1960. *The Philosophy of Sin: And other studies on the problem of man's moral life*. Marshall, Morgan & Scott: Hants UK

Hebrews 2:7-8 points out that though angels were created before mankind and presently hold a higher position than man, mankind will be judging angels (1 Corinthians 6:3; Hebrews 2:5) in the Kingdom of God to come. They are not in the image of God and therefore, cannot represent God as human beings can. Human beings are the only beings created in the image and likeness of God (Genesis 1:26) with the capacity to produce/bear spiritual fruit for God. Jesus died for mankind's redemption and not for that of angels (2 Peter. 2:4; Jude 6).

Isaiah 14 and Ezekiel 28 make references to Satan in all his glory, splendour and eventual dethronement. It is shown in Ezekiel 28, that Satan was not an ordinary being. As a ministering spirit being, he did indeed have control and power over the earth. He was in Eden, the Garden of God, and was acquainted with the purpose of God for mankind. Notice verse 14 of Ezekiel 28 that he was the anointed cherub who covers and was in the seat of government. His task was to guide humanity to the knowledge of why they were created. (Satan's character test) God's intention is to increase the community of beings (Family of God beings) who would carry out His task for the universe. God wanted a set of beings that He could tabernacle with, and thus, would elevate the status of mankind above that of angels, including Satan, the anointed Cherub.

In reading both texts one will not readily notice a command (law) in covenant given to Lucifer, the anointed Cherub, like that given to Adam in Genesis 1:28 to . . . *'be fruitful, and multiply; fill the earth and subdue it; have dominion . . . over every living thing that moves on the earth'.* In fact, there is no command given to angels, but based on the fact that they were created "ministering spirits sent forth to minister for those who will inherit salvation" (Hebrews 1:14), suggests a command from God, that required the obedience on the part of angels as it is with mankind. Satan became rebellious to God out of a heart of covetousness, as he did not want to have mankind being elevated above himself. A law suggests that there is an equal and opposite reaction to a stimulus, so the opportunity existed for Lucifer to disobey the Law. Take note of Ezekiel 28:14 in which Satan was a guardian on the holy mountain (government) of God. He was given dominion and power over all in the Garden of Eden and whomever else God would have placed there. Mankind had to be a part of that plan for Satan to rebel in jealousy. Satan was not only jealous of God but also of the fact that mankind would become 'God,' hence his becoming subject to man.

Now, look at Hebrews chapters 1 and 2, which speak to the ministry that is superior to angels. "*Angels as ministering spirits to serve those who are to inherit salvation* (Hebrews 1:7, 14)" conveys that there is more to the status of mankind than that of angels. "The assertion that the angels are sent forth on a mission of service to the heirs of salvation is a logical inference from the biblical text. Angels clearly have their place in the process economy of redemption, but it is not at the Father's right hand."[13] In Hebrews 2:5, one will find God's revealed purpose for creating mankind in his own image and likeness. God did not subject the world to come unto angels but to those of his very nature—man. Mankind, including the Son of God, Jesus Christ (Hebrews 2:9), was

---

[13]   Lane, W. L. 2002. *Vol. 47A*: *Word Biblical Commentary: Hebrews 1-8*. Word Biblical Commentary. Word, Incorporated: Dallas

made lower than angels (*only for a little while*) and would be exalted above them at the appointed time. Satan was not in agreement so he rebelled. He said in Isaiah 14:12-14, "*I will ascend into heaven, I will exalt my throne above the stars of God, I will sit upon the mount of congregation, in the utmost part of the north, I will ascend above the heights of the clouds; I will make myself like the Most High.*'

Satan wanted to "*make himself like the Most High*" because he knew that mankind's destiny is to become like the Most High. Hold it just a minute! Humans as God-beings do not signify that there will be many "Gods" or that deified humans will be taking over the supreme place of the Father, or knock Him off his throne. Oh No! Deified humans will share the very divinity of God as heirs and joint heirs (Romans 8:17), provided they are in obedience to the Law, as Christ the second Adam did. Mankind will be at one with God. Remember, it is God who is reproducing himself through man. It is God who will share His divinity with humans upon obedience. It is the free gift of salvation, divinely designed for man to become God (Psalm 82:6; John 10:32-38). The Father and Son will always be above deified beings but will possess the same divine nature of being as the species of the Godhead. It was Satan's task to see that this was accomplished because he had a command and responsibility from God to make it happen. He felt he had the power to do whatever pleases him and this resulted in him being cast out as a profane thing from the mountain of God. Satan became proud and made a deliberate decision to rebel against God. He forsook his ultimate responsibility. Chambers again commented,

"The sin of Satan is revealed only dimly, but the dim outline indicates that it was the summit of all sin, full, free, conscious, spiritual sin; he was not entrapped into it, he was not ensnared into it, he sinned with the full clear understanding of what he was doing."[14]

There had to be authority/law for Satan to rebel against. Romans 8:7-8; Romans 4:15 and 5:13 make it emphatically clear that there can be no penalty for crimes committed without the rules broken. Not only did Satan rebel but also he wanted to put an end to the structure of government by disobeying Him who was set in authority over him. Re-examine his statement '*I will make myself like the Most High.*' He wanted to be his own boss (God) and not submit to authority. He broke in essence the codified law given to Israel. If the law were not broken it would nullify one of the character traits of God the Eternal; that He is truly a God of Justice. According to Hebrews 2:2, it is by "God's evaluation, every violation and disobedience received its just punishment"[15] and reward. God does not punish anyone unnecessarily as some preachers claim. All suffering is for righteousness sake!

But why would Satan want to covet (first and tenth commandment) the position of God (and man) if he had such authority and power? Clearly, as was noted earlier, Satan knew that man made in the image of God, is the

---

[14]   Chambers, O. 1996, c1960. *The Philosophy of Sin : And other studies on the problem of man's moral life.* Marshall, Morgan & Scott: Hants UK

[15]   Bahnsen. Greg L. (1996) *Five Views on Law and Gospel.* Zondervan Publishing House. Grand Rapids, Michigan 133

only being capable of inheriting salvation and becoming God. Salvation is God's divinity being shared with man. Man will be like the Most High. It is a shared destiny of oneness. Satan's responsibility in helping mankind to reach this attainable goal, for which he was created, brought on jealousy and fear. Fear in scripture is seen as the lack of love (1 John 4:8). He felt that as first created he had pre-eminence over the position that man will receive upon obedience. He feared losing the position that he had been given to 'inferior man' and coveted that of the Most High, because he thought God was unjust. It is no mystery that he wants to see mankind annihilated and will use any means necessary to deceive mankind into believing that he cannot achieve his inheritance. Satan, as a spirit being, in rebelling against God, had an evil spirit that was against the good spirit of His maker (Matthew19:16-17; Mark 10:18). His mind/spirit had conceived his rebellion. He felt that equality with God (Philippians 2:6) was something that mankind should not have and is going about like a roaring lion seeking to devour him (1 Peter 5:8). But God has declared Satan to be a liar and a defeated foe. Satan had no love or reverence for His Lord and Master, spiritual Father and Creator; no regard for authority and God's sovereignty. He had a rebellious, covetous and evil spirit that could not exist simultaneously within the same place and time and this resulted in his banishment.

Covetousness in the Hebrew language is *be'sa,*—"the desire for dishonest gain or selfish desire." In Greek, the word is *pleonexia* and means ruthless self-assertion. In essence, it is the worship of self and is labelled idolatry. Idolatry can be seen "as the placing of another in a position of authority in one's life, that the other does not deserve or merit." It is the placing of "any force, person or thing that becomes paramount" or is given allegiance to in one's life instead of the Highest Authority—God. "It is an aberrant psychological condition that disables an individual from finding his/her own true course"[16] or destiny. It is this idolatrous spirit of the prince of the power of the air (Ephesians 2:2) that is being transferred to mankind. Romans 5:13-14 reads, *"For until the law was in the world . . . nevertheless death reigned from Adam to Moses, even to those who had not sinned according to the likeness of the transgression of Adam . . ."* In speaking of the changeless promise given to Abraham by God in Galatians, Paul mentioned that the law was added because of transgression (3:19). What was the transgression of Adam? Let's find out!

---

16   www.torah.org. Avraham Avinu and the War to free the Minds of Humanity. HaRav Ariel Bar Tzadok (2009)

Sin in the Human Race

Now let's look at sin in the human race as we continue on its definition since it is for the love of humanity (John 3:16) that God came to die so as to reconcile mankind back to Himself. Because of Satan's downfall the earth was *tohu* and *bohu*; (Genesis 1:2) meaning chaotic, and in physical confusion, wasted and empty. This darkness and mayhem that was on the face of the earth was what Satan brought with Him. It "evokes everything that is anti-God: the wicked (Prov 2:13), judgment (Exod 10:21), death (Ps 88:13)."[17] Scriptures declare that Satan has deceived the whole world (Genesis 3:1; 2 Corinthians 11:3; Revelation12:9, 15). However, God not deterred by Satan's actions continued His 'Kingdom Expansion Plan' with humanity by refashioning the earth (Psalm 104:30) making it inhabitable for man. Some of the greatest lessons missed by some are to be found in the first three chapters of Genesis. One such is that Satan, in his rebellion against God over man's elevated position, destroyed man's home. God's intention from the beginning was to tabernacle with man here on earth (Revelation 21:3), not in heaven as is currently purported by some. **Heaven is not the reward of the saved.** The belief is that when believers die they automatically go to heaven, is not supported in scripture. According to the New Catholic Encyclopedia "the general stream of teaching was that heavenly bliss is granted to the disembodied soul immediately after whatever necessary purification follows death."[18] There would be no need for a

---

[17] Wenham, G. J. 2002. *Vol. 1: Word Biblical Commentary: Genesis 1-15*. Word Biblical Commentary. Word, Incorporated: Dallas

[18] New Catholic Encyclopedia (2003) Volume 6, page 678

resurrection if the dead automatically goes to heaven. First Peter 1:4 says our inheritance is reserved in heaven awaiting us. Zechariah 14:4 also declares that God will come down from the heavens in clouds to set up His Kingdom here on earth and in Revelation 22:12 Jesus said He is coming with the reward. This is to fulfil the promise made to Abraham (Galatians 3:9). Note that it was Satan who first mentioned going to heaven. Look again at his declaration Isaiah 14: 12-14 "*I will ascend into heaven, I will exalt my throne above the stars of God, I will sit upon the mount of congregation, in the uttermost part of the north, I will ascend above the heights of the clouds; I will make myself like the Most High.*' Satan is the first one who wanted to go to heaven and many are following his lead. Easton remarks,

> "according to the Jewish notion there were three heavens, The firmament, as "fowls of the heaven" (Gen. 2:19; 7:3, 23; Ps. 8:8, etc.), "the eagles of heaven" (Lam. 4:19), etc . . . the starry heavens (Deut. 17:3; Jer. 8:2; Matt. 24:29) . . . "the heaven of heavens," or "the third heaven" (Deut. 10:14; 1 Kings 8:27; Ps. 115:16; 148:4; 2 Cor. 12:2)."[19]

Those who look to the story of Enoch (Genesis 5:23-24) and Elijah (2 Kings 2:11) for rescue have neglected the declaration of Christ who declared that "*no one has ascended to heaven but He who came down from heaven . . .*" (John 3:13). These texts were simply referring to the atmospheric skies as Hebrews 11:13 affirm that they all died. Scripture says Enoch was translated. *Translated* means to move, transfer

---

[19]   Easton, M. 1996, c1897. *Easton's Bible Dictionary.* Logos Research Systems, Inc.: Oak Harbor, WA

or transport—He was moved to somewhere else where he died at the age of 365 (Genesis 5:23). Elijah was taken up into the atmospheric heavens by a whirlwind; he was not in the heaven. Heaven is the throne of God (Isaiah 66:1). The Old Testament confirmed that Elijah continued to reign after Elisha took over. Note that Jehoshaphat reigned under Elisha and was succeeded by Jehoram. Elijah wrote a letter to Jehoram (2 Chronicles 21:12-15) stating his punishment from God for his evil. This was done after he was taken up in the whirlwind.

Go back to sin in the angelic realm. Satan was in Eden, the Garden of God (Ezekiel 28:13) here on earth before it was destroyed and refashioned by God. Satan's task was to help man in becoming a tenantless home habitable for God; sharing the very essence of His being. Satan not only thrashed man's physical home at that time but his mission continues to the present day to make man's spiritual home uninhabitable for the Eternal. There will be another refashioning of the earth so that mankind can dwell with His maker at the coming Kingdom of God. In Revelation 21:1-3, John on the aisle of Patmos saw a new heaven and a new earth. It came down out of heaven from God—that's what Jesus Christ has gone to prepare (John 14).

Another important oversight by many is the 'lights' orchestrated for signs, . . . seasons, . . . days and years registered in Genesis 1:14. They are passed over as if they hold no significance for God or man, like the reading of the genealogical record in the book of Chronicles. The Hebrew word in verse 14 is *moed* which means festivals; feast days or appointed times. G. J. Wenham explained that "the lights arranged by God carry a 'threefold function of the heavenly bodies, to "divide," to "rule," and to "give light," thus each mentioned twice within the same chapter."[20] These times are calculated by the earth's movement in relation to the sun and moon and determine the time and seasons on the calendar. It is what scientists call Orbital laws. These laws allow for the regulation of the "weather (Matt. 16:2-3); a testimony to the creative work of God (Pss. 8, 19; Rom. 1:14-20); and were and *will* be used also for divine judgment (Joel 2:30-31; Matt. 24:29)."[21] However, these festivals depicted far more than just the regulation of the weather or divine judgement on a calendar counted by the moon or sun. They are universal laws and signs; a guide to man's redemption as a tabernacle being here on earth. It is a great portrayal and celebration of how God chose to reveal Himself to mankind and how mankind can come to know the true and living God; by the signs, seasons, days and years. God's demonstration of love is seen in the annual festivals listed in Leviticus 23; and is the symbolic shadow in the person of Jesus Christ (Colossians 2:16).

The mutuality of the Godhead contemplated fashioning a being endowed with mind and volition; capable not only of rebellion against his creator but having the ability to fulfil the will of God to the highest degree. This being is bequeathed with power and influence over the future of humanity. The atheist who asks why God created man knowing he would disobey Him has simply asked the wrong question, not knowing the purpose of human existence. It is, however, sad that some cannot find answers and has

---

[20]   Wenham, G. J. 2002. *Vol. 1: Word Biblical Commentary: Genesis 1-15*. Word Biblical Commentary. Word, Incorporated: Dallas

[21]   MacArthur, J. J. 1997, c1997. *The MacArthur Study Bible* (electroniced.). Word Pub.: Nashville

subtly been drawn into the promotion of atheistic thoughts and philosophies. Because atheists have chosen not to find answers by being disobedient to the Law (Psalm 10:4), they have opted to find rational emotive solutions that apply to their itching ears (2 Timothy 4:3). God's purpose for creating mankind is for mankind to personify His character and later to be born into the Kingdom of God. In order to replicate the character of God, mankind is given an equal opportunity as God (His Son Jesus Christ), in relation to the law—being made in His own image and likeness. God's character is self-determined by His freewill and choice and those in His image and likeness are equal in terms of choice and opportunity and will be in reward (Colossians 3:4; 1 John 3:2; Romans 8:17; Revelation 21:7). God is equally capable of doing evil as He is of doing good; he created evil (Isaiah 45:7) but His 'good' character is determined by His choice to do good continually.

Again the atheist might feel justified when he states that the great God Almighty created evil. Who would want to identify with a God that does good all the time and doesn't have an occasion to do evil. Because God is great He is able to do both. God is sovereign; he can choose whether or not to act in an evil manner. That's character; that's God. Adam chose to forfeit that opportunity by his choice to disobey God; he went against the law of choosing good (James 4:17). Therefore, God cannot be accused of tempting humanity with sin (evil) (James 1:13-16). Sin came about because man's choice was evil; he went against the Law (of the spirit) that created him; that is, God. Do not be deceived, my beloved, the evil that exists is from His created beings not from God himself—God did not choose evil, man did with the aid of Satan, the devil. The fact that

God created the opportunity for evil does not negate man's free will—God himself counselled man against it (Genesis 2:16-17). The atheists have simply conceived God in their own images and likenesses rather than the other way around. They forget that "in every walk of life a criterion of our love for Christ (*God*), or lack thereof, is keeping His word (John 14:23-24)."[22] They have deemed themselves more loving and compassionate than the Creator who has merely asked one thing of mankind—obedience. Mankind disobeyed and must pay the penalty for breaking the Law. The sovereignty of God demands it and not fools (Psalm 14:1) emotional reasons and logic of what ought to be.

God, as the good parent, has always nurtured his children in the way of the Lord (Ephesians 6:1-3) encouraging them to choose life over death; obedience over disobedience (Genesis 2:15-17; Deuteronomy 30:15-19). In the Garden of Eden there were two trees—the tree of life and the tree of the knowledge of good and evil. Observe that man was not yet in disobedience (still in the image of God though not immortal) and that "explicit permission is given to eat of them all save the tree of knowledge."[23] It was after he disobeyed that he was prevented from continuing to eat of the tree of life (Genesis 3:22-24). Salvation is a free gift (Ephesians 2:8-9; 2 Timothy 1:9). Adam and Eve had access to this priceless gift but lost it. This again proves another particular doctrine to be a blatant lie—*Once Saved, Always Saved.* If Salvation is something we gain without

---

[22] Bahnsen. Greg L. (1996). in the book *Five Views on Law and Gospel.* Zondervan Publishing House. Grand Rapids, Michigan. 116

[23] Wenham, G. J. 2002. *Vol. 1: Word Biblical Commentary: Genesis 1-15.* Word Biblical Commentary. Word, Incorporated: Dallas

the possibility of losing why did God warn against losing one's soul to death in the beginning and why would Christ, in the New Testament, ask the question in Matthew 16:26 *'For what profit is it to a man if he gains the whole world, and loses his own soul? Or what will a man give in exchange for his soul?'*

"Once saved, always saved" promotes the notion that evil has ceased and that character is a onetime development in the life of the believer. The encouragement to continue in the things of the law tells that we can walk out of the path of truth and light and go back in a lifestyle of transgression/ unrighteousness and continue therein to the sneering of the conscience, leaving no room for repentance. Furthermore, there would be no need for a hell (gehenna) because hell is prepared for the lost, unrepentant souls (Revelation 17:8; 20:7-15) and advocates the belief that falling away or apostasy is unlikely. When the scriptures speak of the impossibility to renew again (Hebrews 6:4), it means they had access to the precious gift of eternal life but lost out in rebellion due to their acceptance of the knowledge of evil and a rejection of good (God). William Lane points out "the danger of apostasy *is* real . . . what is signified is not simply instruction for salvation but the renewal of the mind and of life."[24]

God made a covenant with his children in the law and encouraged obedience by letting them know what would be the consequences of their actions. A covenant is an agreement, verbally or otherwise, designed to officially and

---

[24]   Lane, W. L. 2002. *Vol. 47A: Word Biblical Commentary: Hebrews 1-8*. Word Biblical Commentary. Word, Incorporated: Dallas

clearly delineate what God expects of man and what man can expect of God. When a good parent has laid down laws (rules) for his household, he goes about deciphering them to his children so that when the consequences are meted out for not upholding the law, they will not see injustice in the actions of the parent. Note that the fifth commandment is with a promise. Therefore, Adam and Eve disobeyed their parent and lost out on the gift of salvation as heirs (Exodus 20:12). They would have been given eternal life had they not broken the command in covenant and the offer still stands to those who are called to obedience.

Observe keenly what happened in the Garden of Eden. This evil spirit now known as Satan, the Devil deceived Eve into disobeying a direct command from God not to eat of the forbidden tree. Adam and Eve were both beings in the image and likeness of each other. Eve was taken directly from man with Adam declaring that this is now bone of my bones, and flesh of my flesh (Genesis 2:23). Both are needed in the work to accomplish the task set out by God. G.J. Wenham notes that "the divine observation is that something was not right with man's situation and alerts us to the importance of companionship for man. Man needs a "helper matching him." [25] Both were connected from the start with creation not considered completed without a mate for Adam. It depicts God's ideal for relationship—one man, one woman and not the debauchery of homosexuality embraced by societies today. Nonetheless, both share much in common though they differ physically and emotionally. But Adam and Eve were even more in the image and likeness of their

---

[25]   Wenham, G. J. 2002. *Vol. 1: Word Biblical Commentary: Genesis 1-15.* Word Biblical Commentary. Word, Incorporated: Dallas

Creator—in that they were "both naked and not ashamed" (Genesis 2:25). The word 'naked' designates both a spiritual and physical nakedness and not just consciousness of one's sexuality. "This is a strongly positive image, connoting . . . . qualities as innocence, freedom, openness, . . . simplicity and sexual intimacy in marriage"[26] God, the Father and the Word who became Christ, know exactly what each other is thinking; so it was with Adam and Eve. They both were of the same mind and spirit and were aware of each other's thoughts. Notice that Eve gave to her husband who was with her. Their relationship with God and each other was impaired after their disobedience and attempt to cover themselves. The oneness of Adam and Eve was a mutuality that existed first with the Godhead and expected to be seen in the relationship with humanity. It demanded respect and love for each other (Ephesians 5:21) out of reverence for their maker and Lord.

The two trees in the middle of the garden hold significant symbolism—the tree of life represents good; God's gift of eternal life to humanity. It is the deposited portion of God's Holy Spirit in those that are presently called, that have an assurance of salvation; slated to receive His power and essence. It is the proverbial tree that bears good fruit (Galatians 5:22-23)—the spiritual mind of God. One will take note that the tree of the knowledge of good and evil was separate from the tree of life. Keep in mind that Satan was banished because evil and good cannot exist simultaneously within the same time and place; yet here in

---

[26] Ryken, L., Wilhoit, J., Longman, T., Duriez, C., Penney, D., & Reid, D. G. 2000, c1998. *Dictionary of Biblical Imagery* (electronic ed.). InterVarsity Press: Downers Grove, IL

Genesis 2:17 they are combined into one entity. This tells us that it is not the knowledge of good that corrupts man but the knowledge of evil. Evil and good did exist as one but could not manifest itself until Adam and Eve disobeyed God's command not to touch or eat of it. God's forbiddance "was a test of Adam's love for *His Creator whether* he would be obedient to God's will and trust Him for his life."[27]

Once the law was broken, death and corruption took centre stage. This evil inclination (brought death, the enemy of God and man since man was created to inherit eternity) now became paramount until God chose to do a new thing through Abraham to whom he had promised that he would make a great people after his name (Genesis 12:1-3). Therefore, Adam and Eve's transgression was against God and His law; God, by nature, is the law. They broke the law required to fulfil their destiny. For that reason, the law cannot be said to be moral or immoral as Adam and Eve were made morally upright, not knowing good or evil, they had the freedom to choose and they chose. Oswald Chambers states that "the life of nature is neither moral nor immoral; our bodies are neither moral nor immoral, we make them moral or immoral".[28] It is because some perceive the law as moral that they chose to keep only the 'moral' aspects and ignore the first four. Exodus 20:1-8 states: *"you shall have no other gods before Me, you shall not make for yourself a carved image—any likeness of anything*

---

[27]   VanGemeren. Willem A. (1996).In the book - *Five Views on Law and Gospel.* Zondervan Publishing House. Grand Rapids, Michigan. 18

[28]   Chambers, O. 1996, c1960. *The Philosophy of Sin: And other studies on the problem of man's moral life.* Marshall, Morgan & Scott: Hants UK

*that is in heaven above, or that is in the earth beneath, or that is in the water under the earth . . . , you shall not take the name of the L*ORD *your God in vain, for the L*ORD*, will not hold him guiltless who takes His name in vain and remember the Sabbath day, to keep it holy.* James 2:10 declares that *'for whoever shall keep the whole law, and yet stumble in one point, he is guilty of all."* All the commandments of God stand or fall together. Genesis 3:6 says *"she saw that it was good for food . . . took of the fruit . . . and ate"*—an action conceived and done. "It was the internal region of man, the innermost that yielded first; bodily action was last; the first thing that yielded was the mind."[29] They chose within the consciousness of their minds to disobey God and acted on that which their minds conceived (James 1:13-16). It was both a spiritual and literal fruit like an apple or a mango. It is also seed-bearing that kept producing more of the fruit that is associated with disobedience (Galatians 5:19-21). This fruit is uncharacteristic of God and his Holy Spirit and consequently Adam's banishment and man's separation (Isaiah 59:2) from God.

The decision to disobey existed in both parties equally; the act was just first carried out by Eve. Let's reason here, Adam alone bears God image at the outset. As the image of God, he epitomizes the very purpose of creation, "which is to transform the physical world into a dwelling place for the divine".[30] However, in order to fulfil this mandate Adam was to maintain a relationship with God, the Eternal and so promote his authority over the earth. "This relationship

---

[29]   Chambers, O. 1996, c1960. *The philosophy of Sin: And other studies on the problem of man's moral life.* Marshall, Morgan & Scott: Hants UK

[30]   www.torah.org

between God and man is, however, not instantaneous but was Adam's responsibility to initiate,"[31] of his own free will. As God's chosen steward on earth, Adam was appointed ruler (Genesis 1:26). However, in his high-ranking position he ran the risk, like Satan, of becoming arrogant, esteeming himself as 'God' considering himself as complete as his maker. This might not go down well with the male populace as they are convinced that "it's the woman's fault;" and Paul in 1 Timothy 2:14 just seem to confirm such bigotry.

Let's allow the scripture to expose the biases of men. In 1 Timothy 2:14, it states that Adam was not deceived but Eve. Any wonder why God chose to call out to Adam as if He didn't know who first ate of the fruit? Let's look at the text again—it is addressing the issue of *headship role and authority*. It says ". . . *and Adam was not deceived, but the woman was deceived and became a transgressor.*" Look at Genesis 2:16 and examine why Paul would have made such a statement. "*And God commanded the man*": he had a responsibility. He was in a covenant relationship with God as head of the human family to care for his wife and property. Adam had to show his love for God by being obedient. Ephesians 5:25 says husbands are to love their wives as Christ the church . . . that He might sanctify her by the washing of the Word. Christ submitted His will in obedience to that of the Father. Therefore, Adam could have refused to eat of the fruit which in turn would prevent the human race from experiencing death. "Adam's sin was the perfect conscious realization of what he was doing."[32]

---

[31] www.torah.org

[32] Chambers, O. 1996, c1960. *The philosophy of Sin: And other studies on the problem of man's moral life.* Marshall, Morgan & Scott: Hants UK

His responsibility was to his head—his God and Lord; (not to his wife Genesis 3:17 or his desires) his duty was to submit to the command of God in obedience as Christ did. Christ sanctified the church by being obedient to every word spoken by God the Father. When tempted by Satan the devil (Matthew 4), Christ overcame by acknowledging what the Father said. He was not deceived into believing Satan's lies. He gave up His need for power to submit to the will of the Father.

Adam did not submit to the authoritative command of God to *"not eat of the fruit",* (Genesis 3:11). It was not the act of the woman but that of the man who was given a direct role as head of the human family that sealed the fate of humanity. Interestingly enough, Adam, with his ego, did not acknowledge he was wrong but blamed God for placing temptation (the woman) in his way (Genesis 3:12-13). Because the woman was deceived, God decreed that the seed of the woman (Genesis 3:15) would crush the head of the deceiver, becoming victorious. God was simply establishing headship role and authority for the home and symbolically the church and not a belittling of the status of women. Therefore, a woman has equal rights to choose based on knowledge, she must seek wisdom and must be careful not to be deceived in her quest. Adam as head did not act in love for God or his wife when he disobeyed the commands of God, hence the need for the second Adam.

The name "Adam" can refer to both sexes and, therefore, indicate that together they were given similar responsibility in terms of dominion over the care of the earth. Both were familiar with the purpose of God and were equally and intimately tied to each other in the process of salvation;

individually both were chastised. However, Adam had the naming rights of all that preceded him and Eve (Genesis 2: 19-23). His naming of the woman signifies headship role and authority. He was now her head and had the responsibility of taking care of her as Christ, the second Adam, would the church—His woman who bears His name. The woman has a role of submission but so is the man. God is the head of the church and family therefore, man should not assume a domineering role. They should show mutual love and respect to each other knowing that both bring to the table something to promote the spiritual, emotional and physical wellbeing of the other in oneness and that both will inherit the same fate. Jesus Christ submits to the Father but is not dominated by Him. God the Father and His Son Jesus Christ work to the fulfilling of the mission to be accomplished and so should mankind. Thus, Adam in participating in the act of disobedience negated his responsibility as head and did not act in love by correcting/rebuking Eve when she presented him with the fruit of good and evil. There is no indication that Adam said "stop, in the name of love" he just went along; both coveted the power of God. Adam's failure led to the second Adam, in the person of Jesus Christ, to fulfil where he failed. This is a designation for leaders in the Churches of God to lead their households well and also to see to it that the assembly (household of faith) does not come under the influence of the enemy. Adam didn't need an excuse; he was in conscious disobedience/rebellion against the covenant of God (Hosea 6:7). He became faithless to his Creator and Lord as head of the human family. Mankind failed in his responsibility which was commanded him by God and became the spiritual property of Satan (John 8:44). In like manner Adam's son, Cain followed the same path (Genesis

4:9) and so has the rest of humanity (except Jesus Christ, the second Adam) incurring the death penalty (Romans 5:12).

Some teach that Adam sinned because he wanted to be God. Yes, he did! He coveted the power of God. Adam coveted his future destiny; he did so out of rebellion as Satan the devil. In order for anyone to inherit the eternal gift of God—the character of 'good' will have to be formed—this comes through tests that require obedience; Adam chose evil (death). Obedience signifies love for God and is life. Jesus the Christ said in John 14:15 "*if you love Me, keep my commandments*"—the character test. It's the choice we all have to make. Satan was the first to teach mankind that the wages of sin (disobedience) does not equal death (Ezekiel 18: 4, 20; Romans 6:23) which has manifested itself in the widely held belief in the *immortality of the soul* doctrine. The belief is that human beings are physically mortal, but spiritually immortal. This has no scriptural support. He used the very object of their affection—their hope—to deceive them; allowing them to question the integrity and truth of the word of God.

Man being made in the image and likeness of God is not a justification for the immortality of the soul doctrine currently purported by some. The fact is that man was made from the physical dust and was basically dead until God blew the breath of life in him. Man **only** became a living soul (*nephesh*) after the fact, not before. Immortality is a gift to be had upon obedience to the call of God, not something we are born with. God Himself declares in Genesis 3:19 that man shall return to the dust from which he came. "*In the sweat of your face you shall eat bread, till you return to the* *ground; for out of it you were taken: for dust you are, and to dust you shall return."* It is the breath of life that gives man consciousness, the ability to think and reason as God. This consciousness is the conscience within man given by the Spirit of God. When one chooses to act in sin he violates the conscience—because he (goes against the knowledge of good) has thought about the good and evil of his actions. Adam killed his conscience with his action. Therefore, when one dies physically or spiritually he is in a state of unconsciousness—dead until the resurrection or call to life by God. Man can be alive in body but his consciousness can be dead to the truths of God and until God awakens that mind through the 'call' he is still dead in his trespasses and sins (Ephesians 2:1). Clearly, man does not have an immortal soul and Ezekiel 18:4 and 20 affirm 'the soul who sins shall die. Sin has deemed all souls dead because all souls came from the first man—Adam. However, mankind desires immortality (Ecclesiastes 3:11) but this immortality is granted to the obedient as Eternal Life to come. Man is presently mortal—flesh and bones. It is the glory (Romans 3:23) of immortality that mankind fell short of at the beginning that is now presently being restored through the call, repentance and the gift of God's Holy Spirit.

Humanity's first love wasn't sin but God. They simply became idolaters after being led to believe that God was supposedly hiding something from them that they desired. Mankind became skeptical of God,

> "the Bible reveals that human nature possesses an incurable suspicion of God . . . that was how sin was introduced to the world, . . . which can never be altered

apart from the atonement because it is connected with the great supernatural power behind".[33]

They both sought their own interests. They both coveted power. Satan coveted the power of God and so did Adam and Eve. If not, why is Adam's coveting power compared to the second Adam Jesus Christ who according to Philippians 2:5-8 did not consider it robbery to be equal with God? Satan said (v5). *"Your eyes will be opened, and you will be like God, knowing good and evil."* Their eyes were indeed opened as Satan pronounced and God Himself declared that the man has become like one of Us, to know good and evil (Genesis 3:22) meaning that they are now like God in terms of choice; not immortality. Only God has immortality (1 Timothy 6:16). In order to be like God or to have God's immortality one will have to make the same choice that Christ made—choosing good over evil. This is why the law is necessary in the plan of salvation. It is the process through which God's character is replicated—one cannot choose good over evil if there is no knowledge of both to choose from. Knowledge of sin comes through the law (Romans 7:7-12) Adam's sin was a conscious revolt against God. It is the foundation of all sin that has been working itself through the human race as people rebel against the commands of God. Consequently, whichever of the commandments that is violated, we will get the characteristics that were in this first sin, the principle of rebellion or idolatry.

---

[33] Chambers, O. 1996, c1960. *The Philosophy of Sin: And other studies on the problem of man's moral life.* Marshall, Morgan & Scott: Hants UK

God declared that all that He had made was very good—including man—Genesis 1:31; Ecclesiastes 7:29. It was man who chose evil by freewill. They felt that if they disobeyed God and ate of the tree of which He distinctly commanded them not to; they would have gotten that which He was supposedly hiding. (No such luck). But how can one get what God has promised if he disobeys; when the prerequisite is obedience? (Man's logic). Satan used the authority of God's name to make his plea and today many proclaim a '*Gospel*' in the name of God that is hell bent on disobedience to the true and living God. Isn't this deceiving one's self? It is in obedience that one will gain what God has promised—life—not the other way around.

Oh what deception! Satan was only pushing his agenda because he wanted to have more souls becoming unfaithful and rebelling against the Almighty. Satan led mankind to believe that God could not identify or did not want to identify with them by hiding truth from them. God has never hidden the truth from man about his true identity and destiny. It is man that is trying to hide from God the true nature of his state. When God called out to Adam after he sinned (Genesis 3:9), it was a '*call*' to repentance, for 'man' to acknowledge his state. According to G. J. Wenham "the Judge of the whole earth is calling man in order to demand an account of his conduct."[34] However, he didn't but hardened his heart to blame the true and living God. Adam and Eve could not come into God's presence as they used to—all naked and unashamed before their Lord and Master; they felt detached. Nonetheless, God had compassion on man

---

34 Wenham, G. J. 2002. *Vol. 1: Word Biblical Commentary: Genesis 1-15*. Word Biblical Commentary. Word, Incorporated: Dallas

(Oh what manner of love!) and extended '*grace*' by making a covering for them on their behalf. This grace was not extended for mankind to continue in sin (Romans 6:1) but to lead to *repentance* and life. Because Adam and Eve were in the flesh it was easy for them to believe such deception, they saw only the physical and sought to satisfy its lust by being disobedient. They felt they could not represent God here on earth. God sees differently, because they are in His image and likeness. He brought forth man in the Spirit of love through which He exists, to live by that same spirit of love as He and His Son.

God believes mankind can accomplish such a task. Notice what God said in Genesis 3:22, "Behold, the man is become as one of Us, to know good and evil . . ." Take note that the text did not say '*man is become like Us*' but '*as one of Us*'—a revelation that the incarnated Jesus Christ pre-existed His human birth. Man has to become like God in terms of choice (spiritual mind of being)—while God had to become like man in the flesh (sin) in order to fulfil the just requirements of the Law. First Corinthians 5:21 declared that, *"He made Him who knew no sin to be sin for us, that we might become the righteousness of God in Him."* This means Jesus lived a life of righteousness to the spiritual and codified aspects of the law to demonstrate His love for the Father and humanity. It is the belief that fleshly human beings can become spirit beings and vice versa. God, in love, created all by His Spirit and is giving mankind that same choice, with equal opportunity that His Son had, to become equal with Him. The whole world will be given this opportunity; therefore, the view that some are pre-destined to be lost without knowing what the truth is negates the justice and love of God.

In first Timothy 2:4 Paul mentioned that prayers and supplications be made for all men because God "*desires all men to be saved and come to the knowledge of the truth.*" If God so desires, it simply means that all men must be given the chance to choose between good and evil. Because of sin, mankind knows and practice evil until the call of God awakens his spirit to the good it was created to be in harmony with. Not that mankind is without an excuse for not seeking after God (Romans 1:18-23); "human beings are culpable before God because they know God *but* forsake the worship of the one true God and turn toward idolatry."[35] Those that will be lost in the end are those who have heard and tasted the truth of the living God (Hebrews 6:6; 10:39) but chose to reject the truth for some reason. The reward of Eternal life makes no sense, or, as a matter of fact, does not exist if the choice whether or not to sin does not exist. Recall that sin is the transgression of the Law.

Adam and Eve had access to the tree of life—the proverbial tree that bears the spiritual fruit of righteousness; all things that pertain to life and godliness (2 Peter 1:3). Unfortunately, with the aid of the devil (Genesis 3; Revelation 12:9), they were influenced to believe otherwise and didn't guard their hearts with all diligence but allowed the enemy to sow seeds of doubt in their minds. Their choice then wasn't for life but death: physical and spiritual death. Mankind became suspicious of God by accepting slanders against Him brought on by the enemy. They failed to live by every word that proceeded from the mouth of God (Deuteronomy 8:3; Matthew 4:4).

---

[35] Schreiner. Thomas R.(2003). *Romans*. Baker Book House Co. Grand Rapids, Michigan. 275-276

Spiritually, man is dead until *called* by God to awaken; Satan the devil holds his identity captive. Since that very first act of sin mankind has been given the task to forsake his idolatrous ways and learn to trust and believe in the true God of the universe. This can only be done through the gift of God's Holy Spirit which He gives to those who obey Him (Acts 5:32). Nevertheless, God, in love through His Son Jesus Christ, moved toward us through the incarnation by setting himself the task to redeem mankind through the shedding of His own blood. Christ died to the flesh so He could live according to the Spirit and is thus calling mankind unto repentance so that they too can live according to the just requirements of the law—the spirit of the law. This is accomplished through God's Holy Spirit which enables and opens one's mind to be guided by the spirit of the Law and not the letter of the Law (2 Corinthians 3:6).

After examining all the information on sin, beginning with Lucifer and subsequently man, one can conclude that sin is a universal, spiritual matter of the mind that stems from idolatry or covetousness. In referring to Lucifer, Ezekiel 28:15 states—'till iniquity was found in you'. Satan consciously chose to rebel against God and has taught this lesson well to humanity as seen in James 1:14-15. It is within the spirit of the mind that sin originates—the consciousness of man. Therefore, when the Bible declares that the wages of sin is death (Romans 6:23), it speaks first of the death of the conscience—the mind that is hostile to God's truth (the good) it knows. James 4:17 says, '*therefore to him who knows to do good, and does not do it, to him it is sin.*' Remember God had to banish Satan because evil and good cannot exist simultaneously in the same time and place and He did the same with mankind (Genesis 3:23). God wants mankind to be like Him by choosing to do good thus His aim is to reconcile us to Himself. Reconcile means to bring into alignment and balance. Why would Christ willingly give up divinity to reconcile man to Himself if the destiny of man is not to become God, to personify His image? God became man so that man can become God.

Therefore, anything that goes against the law of good for both God and humanity is a transgression against the law (1 John 3:4) and is termed as sin. It is the selfish act of covetousness which the Bible declares as idolatry (Ephesians 5:5; Colossians 3:5); the evil that God will destroy for the purpose of good. God, in love, created the universe with mankind in His own image and likeness and promised eternity upon obedience to His Word. Adam out of greed for power disobeyed God's command and Jesus Christ, the second Adam, fulfilled that law of love for humanity by His obedience. However, because God, in His foreknowledge knew that man would have sinned, God, the Father covenanted (Titus 1:1-2; Acts 2:22-24) with the 'Word'—His Son, Jesus Christ to be the spiritual solution to man's dilemma. John 3:16 reveals *For God so loved the world that he gave His only begotten Son, that whoever believe in Him should not perish but have everlasting life*. This requires the repentance of mankind for disobeying the Law by believing in God through the person of Jesus Christ who not only gave the Law with His own mouth but also lived it perfectly (Hebrews 5:9).

Seeing that sin brought death to man, it is man who needs rescuing, so let's examine God's solution for mankind.

The Solution for Sin

In examining the definition and root cause of sin, it became evident that sin is a universal, spiritual matter of the mind and consequently, requires an equally universal spiritual solution. The law was broken because of unbelief/idolatry on the part of Adam and Eve. They failed to take God at His word. This lack of faith exhibited in the first Adam was shown to be complete in the second Adam—Jesus Christ. Mankind failed to uphold the law by not imitating the character of God and thus in order to replicate God's character of love, one needs to have faith in the giver, sustainer and upholder of the law. This person is none other than God whose expressed image is found in the incarnated Jesus Christ. Therefore, the solution to sin lies within man's choice in showing forth that love. He said 'if you love Me keep My commandments' (John 14:15). Mankind made a conscious decision within his mind (the seat of his thoughts and beliefs) to disobey God. It is within the mind that actions of faith or faithlessness are conceived and that is where repentance must also begin. Arthur W. Pink echoed that "the best way to keep men from committing sin in act is to keep them from desiring it in heart."[36] Mankind needs a change of heart/mind in order to serve the true and living

---

[36] Pink, A. W. 2000. *The Ten Commandments* (electroniced.). Ephesians Four Group: Escondido, CA

God. He needs to repent and believe the Gospel (Acts 2:38; 3:19).

Repentance is a turning away from to a returning to. According to Rugh,

> **"Repentance means a change of mind**, with reference to sin, self, and God. It is an act of faith, the result of a conviction inwrought by the Holy Spirit through the preaching of the gospel. Jn. 16:7-11; Rom. 10:9-18. True repentance affects the mind, the heart or the emotions, and the will of man."[37]

Already established is the fact that man, in disobedience, turned away from God and through the '*call*', God is asking man to return unto Him. God is not calling everyone now but a select few, just as He did with the nation of Israel and this is also supported by the reaping of the harvest (Leviticus 23:10; 1 Corinthians 15:20). This repentance is for man to believe in God through Jesus Christ not just for the forgiveness of sins (Acts 2:38; Ephesians 4:32) but as the second Adam who condemned sin in the flesh so that the just requirement of the law might be fulfilled in those who walk not according to the flesh but according to the Spirit of the law (Romans 8:3-4). Repentance is an act of faith, the vehicle by which mankind may obtain salvation.

Hebrews 11:1 informs us that faith "is the substance of things hoped for, the evidence of things not seen. It is an assurance that an '*individual* considers a particular claim,

---

[37]   Rugh, W. 1998. *Christ in the Tabernacle: Person and work of Jesus Christ*. Woodlawn Electronic Publishing: Willow Grove, PA

such as God exists, to be actual knowledge—absolutely certain knowledge'[38] (Romans. 8:24; 2 Corinthians 4:18; 5:7). Faith is love in action and Paul in Romans 13:8-10 confirms this by stating '*love is the fulfilling of the law*' (Galatians 5:14; Exodus 20:13-15; Leviticus 19:18; Deuteronomy 5:17-19, 21). God demonstrated this love for us (Romans 5:8) so that all can have access to life in the Spirit. Now there are some who preach and teach that love has replaced the law. This has no evidence in scripture, as 'law and love are not opposed but complementary.'[39] Love cannot replace the law because God himself is the law and is love. If love has replaced the law it simply means that God has replaced Himself who is both love and law, therefore the law still exists. If the law is replaced by anything else, lawlessness has taken centre stage. Greg Bahnsen notes that 'in the teachings of Jesus (as well as of Paul), love does not replace the law . . . but provides a summary statement. A summary does not abrogate that which it summarises'[40] 'for the law in the Old Testament required the same love.'[41] Some have replaced God with lawlessness so they can teach the commandments and doctrines of men (Matthew 15:8-9; Mark 7:7-9).

---

[38]   Edwards, Wesley P: *Understanding Reason and Faith*. Editor@ FreethoughtDebator.com

[39]   VanGemeren. Willem A.(1996). In the book *Five Views on Law and Gospel*. Zondervan Publishing House. Grand Rapids, Michigan. 33

[40]   Bahnsen. Greg L. (1996) In the book *Five Views on Law and Gospel*. Zondervan Publishing House. Grand Rapids, Michigan. 65

[41]   Kaiser, Jr. Walter C. (1996). In the bok *Five Views on Law and Gospel*. Zondervan Publishing House. Grand Rapids, Michigan. 303.

"This claim (*the act of faith*) to certainty is held in the absence of adequate evidence or in direct contradiction to the evidence."[42] It is an active element that requires some amount of physical action, as well as consciousness, and is supported by James 2:14-26 which concludes that faith without works is dead. In order for God to show His love for mankind it had to be demonstrated in the actions of His Son Jesus Christ. The requirement is no less for the saints. Thus faith is a spiritual law like any other law of science that operates on precise premises of immutability, inviolability and universality. Adam and Eve lacked faith on the conscious thought level which fuelled their action on the physical level. They were convinced by Satan to believe a lie. He spoke to their conscience and modified the truth of God so it could look appealing. Both chose to disobey God for their own selfish reasons, and are culpable in every respect as they refused to obey God and instantly entered the snare of Satan. Disobedience or law—breaking occurs when faith is lacking and suspicion (disbelief) about God takes precedence, which does not bring us the reward sought.

The Bibles teaches that the solution to man's problem lies in the forgiveness of sins that God extended to humanity in the form of grace. Grace is the unmerited favour of God to all humanity; and is not a New Testament occurrence. A.W. Pink observed,

---

[42] Edwards. Wesley P. *Understanding Reason and Faith*. Editor@ FreethoughtDebator.com

"The grace which had been behind the law came to light through Jesus Christ so that it could be realized. As a matter of fact, grace had been in operation from the beginning. It began in Eden with the first promise of redemption immediately after the fall. All redemption is of grace; there can be no salvation without it, and even the law itself proceeds on the basis of grace."[43]

Repentance requires the active expression of faith (Acts 2:38) in the person of Jesus Christ. John 3:16-17 is used in support of the claim "*For God so loved the world, that he gave His only begotten Son, that whoever believes in him should not perish but have everlasting life. For God did not send His Son into the world to condemn the world, but that the world through him might be saved.*" Mankind's reconciliation and salvation rest in Jesus Christ who was pre-destined before the foundation of the world (1 Peter 2:20; Titus 1:2; Acts 2:23). As in Adam all died so in Christ all will be made alive (1 Corinthians 15:22). God made special mention of this '*Good News*' of man's redemption from sin in Genesis 3:15 where the promised Messiah, through the seed of the woman would crush the head of the serpent. But why is it necessary to hold a belief in Jesus Christ? The answer is simple. It was this Jesus Christ (God) who was with the Father that Adam and Eve failed to believe in at the beginning (John 1:1-3).

Let us examine Genesis 3 again: the scene in which Satan, the devil, tempted Adam and Eve. In verses 3-5 the conversation between Eve and the serpent reads, . . . "*but of the fruit of the tree which is in the midst of the garden, God*

---

43   Pink, A. W. 1999. *The Law and the Saint.* Logos Research Systems, Inc.: Oak Harbor, WA

has said, You shall not eat it, nor shall you touch it, lest you die. Then the serpent said to the woman, You will not surely die: for God knows that in the day you eat of it your eyes will be opened, and you shall be like God, knowing good and evil." Notice the choice of words "*You shall not eat it, nor shall you touch it, lest you die,* but Satan said "*. . . You will not surely die.*" At first glance it would seem like Satan was right and that God was actually deceiving them. Notice he said that she would not surely die but added "*for God knows that in the day you eat of it your eyes will be opened and you will be like God knowing good and evil.*" This is what caught their attention-the opening of the eyes to be like God. Their eyes were indeed opened but they discovered that they were naked. Satan knew the plan of God—to elevate mankind to the status of divinity. He also knew that they feared death, the enemy of humanity (because God has placed the desire for immortality in men's heart Ecclesiastes 3:11) and were deceived into believing they "*will not surely die.*" It wasn't their desire to be like God that killed them, but their desire to go against God in getting it. They became idolatrous in their desire. It is evil and good that cannot tabernacle in the same place. Remember eternity is the gift of obedience. They did die physically and spiritually. Adam physically died when he was 930 (Genesis 5:5) but their spiritual death was almost immediate. Wenham mentioned that

> the "expulsion from the garden was an even more drastic kind of death . . . they did die on the day they ate of the tree: they were no longer able to have daily conversation with God, enjoy his bounteous provision, and eat of the tree of life; instead they had to toil for

food, suffer, and eventually return to the dust from which they were taken."[44]

This fear of death stemmed from a lack of faith in the Word of God, the promise of God the Eternal in granting them immortality upon obedience. These potential "God-beings" wanted their inheritance like the prodigal son of Luke 15 before it was due. As flesh and blood individuals, they had limitations and wanted more, coveting the power of the Eternal. The desire to have more is not a sin in itself, it becomes a sin when it takes priority over the word of God. Covetousness is the sin of idolatry (Ephesians 5:5; Colossians 3:5) and it stems from dishonesty, greed and selfishness. They desired more. Like Satan they sought to be like the "Most High" out of rebellion and a dishonest and selfish manner.

Adam and Eve aspired to be like the Most High and as the saying goes, "the proof of the pudding is in the eating." They ate doubting God and destroying their own identity and destiny. They lost out on eternal life which would have eventually been granted to them after successfully passing the test of obedience (choosing good over evil). This test of love requires that mankind obey God and do good (Romans 2:7). God tests us to know what is in our hearts. His "will demands a response in obedience . . . . and obedience must come from a believing heart."[45] He said if you love me keep

---

[44]   Wenham, G. J. 2002. *Vol. 1*: *Word Biblical Commentary : Genesis 1-15*. Word Biblical Commentary . Word, Incorporated: Dallas

[45]   VanGemeren Willem A. (1996). In the book Five Views on Law and Gospel. Zondervan Publishing House. Grand Rapids, Michigan. 202.

my commandments (1 John 5: 2-3) and the command was not to incorporate evil with good. It is demonstrated through faithfully accepting the word of God as truth. Love for God means that He is honoured above all else—that 'no other gods *be* before *Him*' (Exodus 20:2)—including self. Sin is ultimately about idolatry. Some claim that Adam's idolatry was his wife; this is yet to be confirmed in the New Testament. Go back to first Timothy 2:14. Idolatry is about worship; an act of obedience that is performed and can be seen. The root cause (of idolatry) is disobedience that manifests itself in doubt and fear and the fulfilling of one's desire over the authority of God. This is the giving of power in allegiance to something or someone (self) who is not worthy of it. Notice that sin is the result of one trying to enjoy the world to come while in the here and now. They wanted more. Okay, let's look at the text. Genesis 3:6 said Eve sought after wisdom. But what did Adam seek? If Eve ate and gave to her husband who was with her, it means that he was aware of what was happening but didn't question his own actions as he desired to partake as much as Eve. Again the evil desire of Satan is transferred to mankind through the conscious power of spirit. Remember also that character is reproduced by obedience to the spirit of a particular law. Adam, being the first created, esteemed his position to be "God" and, therefore, gave allegiance to his desires rather than God's. No other god including self must be before Him. It stems from covetousness, which results in fear and the negating to do the will of God the Eternal. Satan transformed/turned the truth of God into a competition (blame game), which the couple also experienced immediately after submitting to his evil desire. Mankind, since then, has never seen each other as equal.

This violation of the Law required that they die (Romans 6:23). God had said *'you shall surely die'*, which was the penalty for the breach. This death was of the conscious soul in rebellion eventually leading to the physical death (Genesis 3:19). The test of Faith is what was needed to fulfil the purpose of the law; and to express their love for God. Keep this concept in mind—faith is a law, like the conduits of electricity. If conducted within the boundaries one is safe, it will perform well and is dependable. On the other hand, if this law is broken, it can and will kill (destroy) you like any other violation of law-breaking. Romans 6:23 declares *the wages of sin is death.* Faith carries with it certainty; certainty carries with it absolute and absolute carries with it truth for which there is no defence. Earlier it was noted that the claim to certainty is held in the absence of adequate evidence. For the first human family there was no evidence that man could become God and they were curious and so is the rest of humanity. The story of doubtful Thomas in John 20:24-29 is a prime example. Christ said *"Blessed are those who have not seen and yet have believed."* Although they (Adam and Eve) were taught and had access to the tree of life, they chose to give dominance to the flesh (natural man) instead of the spirit (spiritual man). They chose to place their hope in the flesh (what they could see) instead of the spirit, not realizing that ' . . . hope that is seen is not hope' (Romans 8:24). They did not have faith in what they could not see (Hebrews 11:1). Therefore, giving precedence to the flesh, they broke the law. "Faith arises when a person lets himself be convinced by God, and so attains a certainty which is objectively grounded and which transcends all human possibilities in its reliability."[46] They failed to believe that flesh and blood (humans) are created in the image and likeness of God, and that from the dust of the earth could actually become immortal spirit beings (1 Corinthians 15:53-54). Thus, when the law speaks of being spiritual it does so because it demands something more than mere obedience of external conduct. It is given through spirit and can only be fulfilled through spirit—the spirit of a true heart (Psalm 51:6) and was never intended to be a means of salvation. Within the mind they doubted, it seemed impossible. They feared death, (love does not carry fear with it—1 John 4:18), but was caught in its net by the very author of it. Man failed to uphold the spirit of the law and to taper his unbelief, God the Father sent His Son Jesus Christ in the likeness of sinful flesh (Romans 8:3-4) to fulfil the just requirement of the law. "It is not that fulfillment of the law's requirement was merely the result (surprising or accidental) of Jesus' mission and death; it was rather God's purpose in sending his Son in the first place."[47] Christ, the second Adam, showed how the law can indeed become flesh and vice versa by His resurrection from the dead; substantiating the hope of all humanity (1 Corinthians 15:13-19).

God loved man so much that He was willing to risk losing His only begotten Son, Jesus Christ, to show the evidence of truth. (John 3:16) Jesus Christ became the atoning sacrifice for mankind's salvation fulfilling the law

[46]   Lane, W. L. 2002. *Vol. 47B*: *Word Biblical Commentary: Hebrews 9-13*. Word Biblical Commentary. Word, Incorporated: Dallas

[47]   Dunn, J. D. G. 2002. *Vol. 38A*: *Word Biblical Commentary: Romans 1-8*. Word Biblical Commentary. Word, Incorporated: Dallas

where Adam failed. His demonstration was an act of love not just for humanity but also for God the Father (John 3:35, 5:20a). First John 3:1-3 expresses this well—"*Behold what manner of love the Father has bestowed on us, that we should be called children of God! Therefore the world does not know us, because it did not know him. Beloved, now we are children of God; and it has not yet been revealed what we shall be, but we know that when He is revealed, we shall be like Him; for we shall see Him even as He is. And everyone who has this hope in Him purifies himself, just as he is pure.*" The only way man will see God as He is, is when he is clothed with immortality, as flesh and blood cannot inherit the Kingdom of God (1 Corinthians 15:50). Smalley in commenting notes that the "lavish" nature of God's love is indicated by the fact that he, as Father, is the author of spiritual sonship and those who acknowledge him, that is to say, can be "called God's children" (2:22-23).[48] There is no other hope of greater value given to mankind than being fully transformed in the image of God as dear children through the power of His spirit.

It is in knowing who God is through the person of Jesus Christ that will help humanity bridge the gap created by the first Adam. But how does one get to know Him? The answer lies in time. It takes time to get to know someone and God is no exception. Mentioned earlier is that God would have revealed himself through the seed of the woman, the promised Messiah, at a point in time to redeem man. The time is none other than the seasons of the Messiah. These seasons are signs and signs are for

---

[48]   Smalley, S. S. 2002. *Vol. 51: Word Biblical Commentary: 1,2,3 John*. Word Biblical Commentary. Word, Incorporated: Dallas

unbelievers (1 Timothy 1: 8-9) and since all are unbelievers the feast "signs (miracles) provide confirmation of His credentials as the one foreshadowed in the symbolism of the feasts."[49] God chose to set His calendar (Genesis 1:14) in motion so that He could know the season, day and very hour that the Son of God would be made known to mankind. Paul in Galatians 4:4-5 noted: *"But when the time had fully come, God sent forth his Son, born of woman, born under the law, to redeem those who were under the law, so that we might receive adoption as sons".* He was born in sin in order to reveal the love of God in rescuing captive humanity from the slavery of sin. Jesus Christ said in John 14 that he came to reveal the Father and those who believe in Jesus have believed in the Father also; showing the oneness of the Godhead. But how did Jesus Christ reveal the Father? It is, in understanding this that one will come to know the true and living God who sanctifies, because salvation is in the belief that Jesus Christ epitomizes the true God of the universe. (John 17:3) Hebrews 1:3 declares the Son of God, Jesus Christ: "who being the brightness of His glory and the express image of His person, and *upholding all things by the word of his power".* If Jesus Christ is the embodiment of God the Father, let's travel through time to see who He is.

---

[49] McQuaid, E. 1986. *The Outpouring: Jesus in the Feasts of Israel.* Moody Press: Chicago

God Revealed by Jesus Christ is...

There is an imbalanced truth that is being preached as it pertains to the salvation process of humanity. We are told to believe in the Lord Jesus Christ and we will be saved (Acts 16:31a) but who is He and why do we need to express faith in Him. The Word of God has revealed to us the true nature and character of the God of the universe and that all can come to know him. However, the criterion set out by God for us to know him differs from that which is purported in some theological circles today. The nature of God as professed by some proponents, in most cases, is limited to the Trinitarian dogma (that began surfacing around AD 325 or earlier) that recognizes the Divine as God the Father, God the Son and God the Holy Spirit. Scripture is in agreement that God is all three yet not three; as an infinite God cannot be limited to numbers. Thus, the nature of God as defined by some does not delineate who He is. Genesis 1:1 and John 4:24 declare the nature of God to be Spirit. First John 4:8 and 16 tells us that God is love. Limiting Him to numbers only confines the reproducing power of God that John says (1 John 2: 24-25) abides in us. In addition, the assigned roles of Father and Son appearing in the New Testament are functioning roles designed to aid the relationship of God and man in the adoption process. God is Spirit (John 4:24) and can only reproduce through Spirit. His aim is to transform our lowly body to the level of His (Philippians

3:21). If God will transform our body to that of His, it is therefore, resolutely clear that the destiny of mankind cannot be disputed. Paul in Romans 6:5 states, *"for if we have been united together in the likeness of His death, certainly we also shall be in the likeness of His resurrection".* How was Christ raised and with what body?

Now for us to understand who God is and the love He demonstrated for humanity (Romans 5:8), we would have to look at the second Adam—the human person of Jesus Christ who fulfilled the very law Adam failed to keep.

Now let's find out who God is!

Scripture has revealed that the character and nature of God is expressly shown through Jesus Christ the Son. However, because mankind has limited God to numbers, they have failed to see how Jesus Christ truly revealed the true identity and nature of God the Father. In first John 4: 8, 16 the author declares that "God is love" and if Jesus Christ is the express image of God the Father, how did He reveal His nature and personhood here on earth? This is no minor matter as salvation is said to be in none other (Acts 4:12). Jesus Christ himself boldly declares in John 14:6 that *"I am the way, the truth, and the life. No one comes to the Father except through Me;"* meaning that Jesus is *the way t*o the Father, the door or entrance (John 10:7-9). He went even further by saying to Philip who asked to be shown the Father, *"he who has seen me has seen the Father" (v9).* Jesus Christ has revealed the nature and character of God the Father; fulfilling His command. Let's examine scripture and see the truth of who God is because humanity is reconciled to God through Jesus Christ (Romans 5:10) who was one with the Father (John 10:30), forgave sins and existed for all eternity.

The Sabbath

Jesus Christ is the Sabbath Rest

The God who created mankind in his own image and likeness chose to reveal himself by the very time that tells mankind who He is. He chose to reveal himself in time—through the Day on which he rested. After creating mankind God first reveal himself to his created beings on the seventh day when he ceased all his labour and creative activities. This shows the very first purpose of the day that the Lord hallowed and sanctified (Genesis 2:2-3). The Sabbath is to be a day of rest for God and his people to commune and have fellowship. This, the Lord of the Sabbath confirmed in Genesis when He met with Adam and Eve in the Garden of Eden and also in the New Testament when he declared, "*the Sabbath was made for man, and not man for the Sabbath. Therefore the Son of Man is also Lord of the Sabbath.* (Mark 2:27-28) It was this day in the Garden of Eden that God communed with his created beings and admonished them in the laws, statues, commandments and judgements to be shared with all humanity. However, because of the failure of the first Adam, God chose to reveal himself to Abraham and the succeeding generations. This he did through the children of Israel. When the nation of Israel went into captivity it was because they had failed to acknowledge the Lord of the Sabbath, subsequently falling into idolatry. The Sabbath Day of rest is the first way in which mankind can begin to know the true God of salvation.

Interestingly, in Christendom today we find that none other of God's commandments cause more contention than that of the fourth—Exodus 20:8 which state "*Remember the Sabbath Day to keep it Holy.*" This word, "remember," shows that 'we are apt to forget Sabbath holiness; therefore, we need a memorandum to put us in mind of sanctifying the day.'[50] The admonition 'remember' indicates that this commandment is not the first association of the Sabbath, but rather a charging to Israel to keep and retain what is already in existence. Why would God instruct the Israelites to "remember" if the Sabbath was not an institution from the beginning? In Exodus 16 it is seen where God expressly showed and tested the faithfulness of his people with weekly miracles and punishments with manna from heaven. Breaking the Sabbath was meted out with severe punishment; it was seen as a matter of life and death. In Exodus 31:15, the Lord declared, *'whosoever does any work on the Sabbath day; he shall surely be put to death.*" It is a sin to break the Sabbath and a sin offering was required of all persons in the Old Testament who profaned the Sabbath unintentionally and death by stoning if intentionally broken (Numbers 15:36).

Look at Nehemiah 9:13-14 which shows how God made the Sabbath known to his people by giving them the laws including the Sabbath. Israel had lost knowledge of it at that time, as some have today but the Sabbath was and still is a part of the covenanted sign of God and his people. This is the second reason God gave the Sabbath. It is a sign between God and His people (Exodus 31:13) and a day of remembering their physical redemption (Deuteronomy 5:15). It was a sign to show that Israel was the nation of God's called out people and to anyone who would accepts

---

the God of Israel (Galatians 3:29). (Read the recorded test in Exodus 16) One must however be mindful that there are a number of Sabbaths referred to in scripture (the annual Sabbaths) all of which show forth the sanctifying sign of the people of God and these are listed in Leviticus 23. If signs are for unbelievers and the Sabbath is given as a sign between God and His people, is it saying that those who do not keep the seventh day-Sabbath are unbelievers and not God's people? And if the Sabbath is a sign, where does it leave those who keep only the seventh day-Sabbath ignoring the annual Sabbaths? Where is the testimony of Jesus Christ, which Revelation 12 speaks of? Revelation 12 tells *it will be a sign of those who keep the commandments of God*, suggesting that the Sabbath is also relevant for the future; a shadow of the coming Sabbath rest of the Eternal. (Hebrews 4) Those who do not keep the Sabbath do not have the testimony of Jesus Christ.

Sabbath in the Bible speaks chiefly of the seventh day of the week, the day on which God rested or ceased His creative work. "The Sabbath day is Saturday. It is the seventh day of the week according to our calendar. Furthermore, the Sabbath day has never been changed to Sunday."[51] Some have not seen that the Sabbath is not only about the Creator resting but also about man and everything else resting on the earth. After the sin of Adam and Eve, even the earth with its animals felt the pinch of the soul that sinned. Genesis 3 noted that the earth brought forth thistles and did not yield her increase in food supply. Everything went out of balance

---

[51]   McGee, J. V. 2001, c1995. *Love, Liberation & the Law: The Ten Commandments* (electroniced.). Thomas Nelson Publishers: Nashville 51.

including the Sabbath Day of rest. When God spoke to Israel, He noted that the "Sabbath was to be a day of rest and refreshment for *them*, their servants, their livestock, and any visitors staying with them (Deut: 13-14)."[52] Bruce Scott notes that "Resting on the seventh day therefore involved more than just physical refreshment. God did not rest on the seventh day because He was fatigued. Rather, the idea of resting spoke more of cessation."[53]

The command in Exodus 20:8 continues by stating, "*Six days you shall labour and do all your work.*" It "denotes that God, the sovereign Lord of our time,"[54] is divinely reminding mankind to remember. The revealed will of God is that man should work and He regulated such time, which was not designed for temporary administration but is continuous. Therefore, the true Sabbath could never be just any day out of seven. Note that in Genesis 2:15 man was placed in the Garden of Eden to tend and keep it. However, he deemed the Sabbath a day of rest for man (Mark 2:27) and not simply for the Jew. This was seen also in Israel's deliverance that those coming out of bondage with them were required to keep it (Exodus 20:10). It was made for the good of all mankind including the Gentile. A further notification is seen in the New Testament where the church is called the Israel of God. (Romans 9:6-8). All will have to follow the Jews' God in covenant relationship.

---

[52] Scott, B. 1997. *The Feasts of Israel* (electroniced.). The Friends of Israel Gospel Ministry, Inc.: Bellmawr, New Jersey

[53] Scott, B. 1997. *The Feasts of Israel* (electroniced.). The Friends of Israel Gospel Ministry, Inc.: Bellmawr, New Jersey

[54] Pink, A. W. 2000. *The Ten Commandments* (electroniced.). Ephesians Four Group: Escondido, CA

The Sabbath was not given to human beings simply to serve as a day of physical rest as is so commonly believed by many. Leviticus 23 enumerates the Sabbath as one of the appointed Feasts of the Lord. The Sabbath is seen as the miniature feast of tabernacle designed to raise the level of human consciousness as to the destiny of mankind. It is in understanding our physical need to "keep the physical day of rest that we will come to appreciate the eternal rest of our souls. Because the Sabbath is observed in memory of creation, it explains human relationship with the Creator that strives for a higher level of human consciousness of what God desires of mankind."[55] At creation, God completed his work in six days. Note that in the Bible, after each time of "action called a day, there was an equal period of inaction called night; yet night was never called a time of rest"[56] neither was it called a Sabbath. The Sabbath therefore, must be seen as more than mere cessation from work-related activities; this symbol of rest is of the Creator—God. The Creator deemed all complete for Himself and mankind. All the pieces fell into place and essentially the Creator was well pleased. Only when everything is in its place and every purpose accomplished can mankind say that there is true rest. "It is when human history is complete that we will all enter into the great Sabbath, where everything on earth would have reached its pinnacle and will be at peace."[57] There is coming a Sabbath rest when all will be at peace, no more death and suffering and this is what our weekly

---

[55] www.torah.org. HaRav Ariel Bar Tzadok. 2008 Secrets of Shabat Observance.

[56] www.torah.org. HaRav Ariel Bar Tzadok. 2008 Secrets of Shabat Observance.

[57] www.torah.org. HaRav Ariel Bar Tzadok. 2008 Secrets of Shabat Observance.

keeping of Sabbath foreshadows. Hebrews 4:1-9 tells there remains a Sabbath rest for the people of God, so people can cease from their works as Christ did from His. How did Christ rest and cease from His works? As we have seen, Christ ceased from his physical work and communed with mankind and with God the Father. Luke 4:16 declared it was his custom.

The weekly Sabbath is observed at the closing of the sixth day (Friday) at sunset and ends at sunset on the seventh day (Saturday) and is commanded by God, to be observed throughout Israel's generations as a perpetual covenant (Exodus 31: 16). This seven-day cycle is a reminder to mankind that all human history is but a cycle and at its conclusion all must be in balance and at peace. Some have claimed that the Sabbath was only for the Jews indicating that the rest is already complete for mankind for whom it was made. However, one must come to accept that the whole world follows a seven-day cycle. Therefore, its relevance is not just to Israel, as all nations of the world are children of God and included in His great plan of salvation for humanity. In Romans 1:18-21, Paul speaks of the awesome majesty and power of God that fills the earth that mankind may be without excuse for not observing His laws. God desires that all men be saved and come to a knowledge of the truth (1 Timothy 2:4) and this begins with an acknowledgement that the Son of man (Jesus Christ) is Lord of The Sabbath (Matthew 12:8; Mark 2:28). What some have purported is that the whole world is not Jewish; therefore, they do not need to keep the Sabbath as the Jews do. One may agree with these proponents, but God is not asking Gentiles to accept the Jews religion but to acknowledge Him as Lord of the Sabbath.

The eternal Sabbath rest is a time when all humanity will come to know and experience God directly; when there will be no more crying, pains, wars and the devil to contend with. Christ demonstrated this in His earthly life and ministry when He freed those held in captivity by the yoke of ritualism (Matthew 23:23). Christ validated his love for humanity by healing people on the Sabbath. (Matthew 12:9-13; Mark 3:1-5; Luke 6:6-10) Thus "the Sabbath is designed to show how good things can get"[58] and the need to do good (Mark 3:4). In Isaiah 66:1, it reads, "*thus says the* LORD: *Heaven is My throne and earth is My footstool. Where is the house that you will build me? And where is the place of My rest?*" God wants to rest with us therefore, asks nothing of us. He does not want what we have (we have nothing) but who we are; who He created us to be. He seeks to create in our hearts a sanctuary for himself, a place where He may rest. God does not need rest. He already rested after completing his good work at the beginning of creation (Genesis 1: 31—2:1-3). This is an indication that though God requires our keeping of the Sabbath our salvation rest is not in keeping with the physical Sabbath, but in God-Our spiritual rest. Thus "in observing the seventh day as holy, man is imitating his creator's example."[59] The Sabbath is deemed a mini Feast of Tabernacles and signifies mankind's ultimate rest at the coming eternal kingdom of God to be set up here on earth. God is not looking for a place where he can merely cease from His labours but seeks a relationship where He can completely envelope and permeate every dimension of our lives, where he can tabernacle and remain

---

58   HaRav Ariel Bar Tzadok. 2008 Secrets of Shabat Observance. www.torah.org.

59   Wenham, G. J. 2002. *Vol. 1*: *Word Biblical Commentary: Genesis 1-15*. Word Biblical Commentary. Word, Incorporated: Dallas

quiet. Mankind no longer enjoyed this relationship as he was separated from God and the abundance that was so readily available to him was now to be gained through toil—of the mind and body.

The Jews however, idolized the physical rituals and aspects of the law by becoming idolaters and not true worshippers. Notice that on a number of occasions Jesus Christ miraculously healed several persons and was accused of breaking the Sabbath (Matthew 12:1-8; Mark 2:23-28; Luke 6:1-5). His aim was to show the spiritual intent of the law hence, His constant rebuke of those who opposed Him. They accused Him of breaking the Sabbath because they fail to acknowledge who and what the day was about—the day symbolized God himself doing good for all. As Lord of the Sabbath, Christ had the authority to correct, re-interpret and even change the way the Sabbath was being kept—instead of changing He magnified it. In Matthew 12, the Jews broke the Sabbath for mere animals who are not in the image and likeness of God, therefore, Jesus challenged their hypocrisy when He answered them by relating 'the biblical story of David and his hungry men eating consecrated showbread reserved only for the priests (Matthew 12:3-4). Although it is not recorded as having occurred on the Sabbath, the action was still a breach of the letter of the law. Jesus also pointed out that on every Sabbath the "priests on the Temple Mount 'broke' the laws against working, and yet God considered them blameless (Matthew 12:5). Further, rabbinical rules allowed for the

Sabbath to be overridden to perform circumcision (John 7:22-23)."[60]

Needless to say, the Sabbath had some prohibitions. However, these prohibitions of forbidden labours, is seen as an "archetypical expression of the ultimate state of human psychological freedom the pinnacle of human development, where humanity is in total harmony with God, the natural world around"[61] himself and each other. Some people do not understand the relationship between the prohibited activities that define the Sabbath and the essential meaning of the Sabbath. If we are to rest as Christ, we must understand a simple yet profound truth. "All our experiences in this physical world come through the mind; what we hear, see, smell, feel and taste."[62] One way we can experience this true element of the reality around us is to rest from our laborious work both on a physical and spiritual thought level. "On the Sabbath the saints must not only remember but also actualize the reality that the ultimate goal and pinnacle of human existence is when all will be in harmony. Therefore, on the Sabbath the ceasing of all distractions, small or great, show a fruit of the Spirit"[63]—self control and restraint that must be practised. God would not want his saints to have personal desires upsetting the delicate balance sought. Note that though mankind was to gain from the land in which

[60] Scott, B. 1997. *The Feasts of Israel* (electronic ed.). The Friends of Israel Gospel Ministry, Inc.: Bellmawr, New Jersey.

[61] www.torah.org. HaRav Ariel Bar Tzadok. 2008. *Secrets of Shabat Observance.*

[62] www.torah.org. HaRav Ariel Bar Tzadok. 2008 *Secrets of Shabat Observance.*

[63] www.torah.org. HaRav Ariel Bar Tzadok. 2008 *Secrets of Shabat Observance.*

he was to tabernacle, he was prohibited from performing certain activities on the Sabbath. "The Bible gives only a few examples of prohibited activity, such as gathering sticks (Numbers 15:32), treading wine presses (Nehemiah 13:15), and carrying loads (Jeremiah 17:21). But the biblical concept of work also seems to imply transacting business, earning a living, or working at a professional occupation."[64]

In Isaiah 1:12-15 God rebuked the people regarding their Sabbath and feast celebrations, not because he was advocating for a cessation of the Sabbath and the Feast Days but because of the hypocritical nature of the people. The people's hands were full of blood and worship to him was not genuine. God could not endure such iniquity any longer and therefore refused to accept the sacrifices offered to Him on the appointed times. Romans 12:9 says *let love be without hypocrisy. Abhor what is evil. Cling to what is good.*" Our coming before God on the Sabbath or Feast Days with bloody hands is an abomination to the great God Almighty, he wants clean hands and pure hearts. Love must be sincere in our worship of God. In Psalm 15 we see the kind of worship that God expects from His people in His tabernacle. God seeks true companionship and integrity in worship so that he may rest and abide with us on the day of rest

Observing the Sabbath is meant to adjust the human consciousness and thought that became imbalanced at the first act of sin. When God's rest abides with mankind, they live in union with the Father as Christ did. Christ thought

---

[64]   Scott, B. 1997. *The Feasts of Israel* (electronic ed.). The Friends of Israel Gospel Ministry, Inc.: Bellmawr, New Jersey

life was enveloped with the presence of God, as the second Adam, and did all that He saw His Father did (John 14:10). For anyone to enter God's rest it requires love to abide (1 Corinthians 13:13); that means in full surrender to His command in perfect trust. Once this is done mankind would have learnt to rest from their labours as Christ did from His (Hebrews 4:10). William Lane notes—

> "The assertion in v 10 stands in a causal relationship to v 9 and clarifies why in the eschatological rest a σαββατισμός will be possible. Whoever has entered the consummation-rest will experience the completion of his work, as did God after the creation (vv 3c-4), and will enjoy the rest that is necessary for the festivity and praise of a Sabbath celebration."[65]

This rest is the ceasing of the turmoil of the soul brought on and caused by unbelief. As the saints seek to obey God through the tests of life, they learn to deal with situations as God would.

In Hebrews 3:8-12, we see a summary statement as to why Israel did not enter the rest of God. He says, *"they always go astray in their heart . . . and have not known My ways. So I swore in My wrath they shall not enter My rest."* Obeying God's way leads to rest. There is no rest in a disobedient, hardened and rebellious heart. Mankind's rest comes from loving God with all his heart and soul (Deuteronomy 5:5; Matthew 22:37) and his neighbour as himself (Matthew 22:39). This calls for the honesty of our

---

[65]   Lane, W. L. 2002. *Vol. 47A: Word Biblical Commentary: Hebrews 1-8*. Word Biblical Commentary. Word, Incorporated: Dallas

souls' needs before the Almighty and allowing the Divine to heal/unleaven us from our evil thoughts. The saints accept this when they follow the example of Christ. In Matthew 11:29. Jesus says *"learn from Me . . . and you will find rest for your souls."* Christ is the ultimate Sabbath rest and when mankind ceases to rebel against God, they will eventually come to rest as He rested. God does not need temples made with hands, but is looking for those who tremble at His word. This is portrayed in Isaiah 66:2, *"but on this one will I look: On him who is poor and of a contrite spirit, and who trembles at My word."* God looks to the man who trembles when He speaks—not a geographic place. Such a man has the Holy Spirit of the Most High abiding in him; the love of the Eternal. He has learned the ways of God; he delights in obedience and has perfect peace, without striving. He has chosen to give God what he asks: nothing less than his all. In return, this man becomes a place, a holy place, where God Himself dwells, a place of rest. God abides in rest; thus, the command to look to Jesus Christ in whom the Father was well pleased (Matthew 3:17) because He will do so for all who yield themselves to Him in like manner.

Now that we have learnt know how Christ revealed himself through the seventh day Sabbath let's see the continued manifestation of Jesus Christ to mankind through the annual Sabbaths.

Passover and Unleavened Bread

Jesus Christ is the Passover lamb and Our Unleavened Bread

Following the fall of Adam and Eve, God did not punish mankind according as the death penalty demands (destroying the human race). He passed over (Romans 3:25) their sin by way of forgiveness in order to show His love and make way for the second Adam—through the seed of the woman (Genesis 3:15) who would crush the head of the serpent. The significance of this "passing over" was not made known fully until the death of Christ the Passover Lamb. The Passover season was originally seen as distinct but came to be observed as one along with the Days of Unleavened Bread in both the Old and New Testaments (Deuteronomy 16:1-8; Matthew 26:17; Mark 14:12; Luke 22:1). Passover began on the fourteenth day of the first month, Nisan while the Feast of Unleavened Bread commenced on the fifteenth lasting seven days until the twenty first day of the month (Exodus 12:15). However, it was the Exodus experience that first shed light on the significance of this event when God chose to put a mark of identity on a people whom He had called through Abraham. It was the preliminary shadow that led to the substance in Christ (Colossians 2:16). This mark of identity is none other than the sign of obedience to a form of leadership or power that will distinguish the saints called by God (Genesis 15: 6; Romans 4:3; Galatians 3:6, James 2:23) and is the sign of all those who walk in obedience to the commands of Abraham's God. Obedience to the commandments of God is a sign/mark of identity (Deuteronomy 6:1, 6-8; 11:18; Revelation 12:17) of the people of God. Failure to keep God's commands is a sign of disobedience and idolatry. Obedience is an act of worship or esteem that we perform to the highest authority (God) by adopting the pattern we see in scripture and the life of Christ. Abraham himself was in idolatry until he became faithful to God by (Genesis 15:7, Nehemiah 9:7, Acts 7:2-4) answering the call to life.

Some will argue that the Passover (like the Sabbath and other feasts of God) was only given to Israel, and that no command was given for its celebration in the Genesis account as a law. One could agree with those who claim that there is no explicit command as a law, but the "seasons" of Genesis 1:14 were set up in anticipation of the sin of Adam and Eve and a revelation and celebration of the Messiah. Christ revealed the Father at an appointed time; a set time. There would be no sign for the wise men to look for if there was no time marker to identify with. Therefore, the function of the Genesis account is not just to tell us how planet earth, with its human and animal life came into existence, but to show that the universal commands of God were also given, hence, the entrance and penalty of sin. The codified law in the form of the Ten Commandments, given after the Passover, was a temporary model set up to lead to Christ (Galatians 3:23-25; Hebrews 10:1) the Passover Lamb (1 Corinthians 5:7). However, the forbidding of partaking of 'evil' indicates that mankind was schooled to know what evil was. If this were not so there would be no reason to punish Cain for killing his brother. The New Testament teaches that the physical aspects of the law were added because of transgression (Galatians 3:19); and given "to human beings who are already under sin (Rom.

3:9)"[66] to be our custodian to bring us to Christ (Galatians 3:24-25). Christ is the master in the school of obedience to whom we must look for liberation by being obedient slaves to righteousness (Romans 6:16). One cannot get to Christ without the law.

As the people on the earth multiplied, the administration of the law changed (NOT THE LAW) and this resulted in the physical codified law on tablets of stone along with the sacrificial rituals and ceremonies. Note the reference to Cain and Abel in Genesis 4 concerning the offering of sacrifices to God. Cain's gift was rejected because he chose to offer fruits instead of a blood sacrifice for sin. Take into consideration that no punishment is given for sin without knowing what the rules are. Also these acts of adultery (Genesis 26:10), murder (Genesis 4:8) and homosexuality (Genesis 19), among others were seen as the breaking of the commandment of God and were deemed punishable even before there was a nation called Israel. Also of note is that we see where Abraham, Isaac and their descendants were blessed for obedience to these laws and commandments, therefore, the law with its interpretation, statutes, judgments and ordinances, which Abraham kept (Genesis 26:3-5), must have already existed before the codified memorial of Exodus 20. The law of God is a covenant between God and man, not Israel. Salvation is not about Israel but about one man and his family. This man is not Abraham but Christ, the true seed (Matthew 1:1), the second Adam who gave his life for His wife (The Church—Ephesians 5:25) in covenant.

---

[66] Moo. Douglas J. (1996). In the book *Five Views on Law and Gospel*. Zondervan Publishing House. Grand Rapids, Michigan. 334

Hosea 6:7 (Job 31:33) informs us that Adam transgressed that covenant with God, unlike Christ who came to do the will of the Father, bringing no condemnation on humanity (Romans 5:16, 18).

In Genesis 1:26-30, the reason for creating mankind is given along with the commands to be . . . *"fruitful and multiply . . . replenish and subdue . . . have dominion . . . and to eat of the produce of the land"*. There must have been instructions in how to carry out these tasks. G. J. Wenham notes, "this command, like others in Scripture, carries with it an implicit promise that God will enable man to fulfill it."[67] Mankind are God's representatives; ambassadors if you may (2 Corinthians 5:20), here on earth upholding the divine principles of law. They were to rule and will see them rule with a rod of iron, those who fail to obey the law. (Revelation 2:27) A law needs interpretation for it to be understood and obeyed and as the people on the earth multiplied the codified law was deemed necessary along with its methods and explanation. The commandment was not just to avoid eating from the tree but to be fruitful and multiply and replenish the earth with that which is in the image and likeness of God. God wants to see the good within Himself (truth and love) be multiplied and bearing fruit in mankind. God wants to see the good reproduced and multiplied in the beings of His nature and kind. The provision for this fruit-bearing was made possible through the access of the tree of life and its verbal/oral command given to the first man, Adam. All came through Adam.

---

[67] Wenham, G. J. 2002. *Vol. 1: Word Biblical Commentary : Genesis 1-15*. Word Biblical Commentary . Word, Incorporated: Dallas

Romans 5:14 notes that *"Death reigned from Adam . . . even to those who had not sinned according to the likeness of the transgression of Adam"* thus, the command to mankind is universal. Thomas Schreiner notes that "as a result of Adam's sin death entered the world and engulfed all people; all people enter the world alienated from God spiritually death by virtue of Adam's sin."[68]

A lamb was slain in order to redeem Adam and to make a covering for humanity's first parents. However, this act must be seen, as far more than a cover for man's physical nudity for which they were quite unconcerned before their disobedience. It is a poignant reminder of their sinfulness or spiritual nudity. The act serves as a cue that God cannot tolerate sin confirming that there can be no atonement for sin apart from the shedding of blood (Hebrews 9:22). The life is seen in blood (Leviticus 17:11, 14) thus, the shedding of blood—the substitution of one's life for another—brought atonement for sins. In the same way, the "Messiah redeemed all of mankind from the bondage of sin by shedding His blood and giving up His life so that we might live (Isa. 53:5)."[69] Another affirmation that the Passover is not about the nation of Israel is that no nation existed at the entrance of sin into the world. Both Israelites and Gentiles came out of Egyptian bondage and received the commandments in a covenant relationship with God. Thus the Passover is about the love that God the Father has for His Son Jesus Christ (the firstborn) and extended to humanity (John 3:16). It is an acknowledgement of the love of God instituted and set

---

[68] Schreiner. Thomas R. (2003). *Romans*. Baker Book House Co. Grand Rapids, Michigan. 275-276.

[69] Scott, B. 1997. *The Feasts of Israel* (electronic ed.). The Friends of Israel Gospel Ministry, Inc.: Bellmawr, New Jersey

up before the foundation of the world (John 17:24; 1 Peter 1:20-21). God forgave and extended grace (John 1:17) to facilitate mankind through His Son Jesus Christ—the Lamb of God who takes away the sin of the world (John 1:29). He made a way for His beloved Son. Christ had to become like those whom He was redeeming (Hebrews 2:14) thus, the need for the incarnation. Because the first Adam died, it required the blood of another to prevent mankind from being annihilated. First Corinthians 15:21-22 states, *for since by man came death, by Man also came the resurrection of the dead. For as in Adam all die, even so in Christ all shall be made alive.*

Animals are souls (Genesis 1:20, 21, 24) and were used in making atonement for sin but their blood was not sufficient (Hebrews 10:4) for man's redemption. The blood that is required to save mankind is that of a righteous soul that consciously thinks and can choose based upon knowledge and freewill hence, the insufficiency of bulls and goats spoken of in Hebrews 10. Hebrews 9:9 speaks of the inadequacy of the animal that could not perfect the conscience (the spirit in man) of the worshipper as the soul of animals are not in cohesion with that of human beings who are made in the image and likeness of God. William Lane comments "the old covenant were unable to provide definitive purgation of the worshiper with respect to conscience."[70] Keep in mind, it is the image of God that human beings are being fashioned into, not animals. Therefore, the sacrifice of God was deemed necessary. Salvation is equally about life, as well as death. Thus, to

---

[70]   Lane, W. L. 2002. *Vol. 47B*: *Word Biblical Commentary: Hebrews 9-13*. Word Biblical Commentary. Word, Incorporated: Dallas

save humanity it required an equal substitute for sin; an equal soul, and God in the person of Jesus Christ, a flesh and blood human, was that perfect replacement. The writer of Hebrews made mention that Jesus Christ had to share in flesh and blood so that through death He might destroy the one who has the power of death.(2:14) The power of death is the spirit of evil associated with the enemy's life. Lane again notes,

> "Since "the children" share a common human nature, "blood and flesh"), it was necessary for the one who identified himself with them to assume the same full humanity. This assertion grounds the bond of unity between Christ and his people in the reality of the incarnation. In the incarnation the transcendent Son accepted the mode of existence common to all humanity."[71]

Salvation requires the death of a soul in order to save (give life to) those souls who are conceived in sin (Psalm 51:5) and given over unto death. Hebrews 9:22 makes it distinctly clear that ". . . , *according to the law almost all things are purified with blood, and without shedding of blood there is no remission.*" Forgiveness of sins came through God (Ephesians 4:32) in the incarnated person of Jesus Christ (Mark 2:5, 10), the Passover Lamb sacrificed for humanity (1 Corinthians 5:7). Some have failed to see the significance of the Passover and the other feast days. They are deemed obsolete and unnecessary but there is no way that mankind can come to know the true and living God without knowing

---

[71] Lane, W. L. 2002. *Vol. 47A: Word Biblical Commentary: Hebrews 1-8.* Word Biblical Commentary. Word, Incorporated: Dallas

who He is as revealed in the feast/holy days that are rich in symbolism.

Oh what manner of love! God in the person of Jesus Christ voluntarily chose to be that Lamb to the slaughter (Acts 8:32). He became man. The living took the place of the one sentenced to death so that man in the end would not die. Thus, God is both man and Spirit and, therefore, denying the humanity of God rejects his saving power and deity and further the destiny of humanity. In 1 John 2:22-23 the author makes it resolutely clear that a liar is the one who denies Jesus is the Christ. It reads (ASV) *"Who is a liar but he who denies that Jesus is the Christ? He is antichrist, who denies the Father and the Son."* The Son is the exact imprint and image of the Father; thus denying one automatically denies the other. It's the law! John 1:1-3, 14 declares the Word was God (Jesus Christ) who became flesh and *tabernacled* among us. Jesus is the "I AM" (John 8:5, 6) who was before Abraham (John 8:58). Thus, the incarnation of Jesus Christ is not a playhouse story for Christmas time but to teach humanity how the redemption of mankind started with the manifestation of Jesus Christ in sinful flesh. Jesus, being God, does not have a genealogical record, because He existed from eternity and those who worship Mary as the mother of God have simply missed this point. Mary is the mother of the human person, not the Eternal God. Also of note: John 3:13 and 6:62, which speak of Jesus Christ as the Son of Man who came down from heaven to give life to the spirit of humanity. It was this Christ, the Passover Lamb, who was made flesh and tabernacled (John 1:14) among us so He could make or be the atonement for mankind's sin.

Because of sin man had to go through a mediator which was the priesthood seen in the ceremonial rituals of the Old Testament. Jesus Christ, the Passover Lamb who acted as High Priest on behalf of Himself and the people—the household of God, now replaces this priesthood. Jesus Christ is that high priest. All can go to God and offer his gift whether he is Jew or Greek . . . slave or free . . . male or female (Gal. 3:28; Col. 3:11) because a change has come to the administration of the law. A change in the administration of the law does not suggest a change in the ultimate plan of God; it is the same plan from the beginning. Go back to the Genesis account and see that mankind was forbidden to eat of the tree of life after they sinned. God chose to put a sword as a form of demarcation between the sinner and access to the tree of life. Bearing the fruits of righteousness would have been easy but now it requires work—hard work.

In celebrating the Passover, according to the Exodus story, a lamb was killed and its blood poured and sprinkled on the doorposts and lintels so as to preserve the first born from death. It was originally a domestic affair carried out by the male-head of the household until the Levitical priesthood, which became old and obsolete (Hebrews 8:13). After Israel's deliverance from Egypt and the subsequent building of the temple, the Passover was celebrated by eating a lamb and pouring out its blood at the foot of the altar along with unleavened bread and bitter herbs (Exodus 12:8; John 19: 28-30). Scott notes that "the biblical commandment not to eat anything leavened during the Feast of Unleavened Bread was so important that God declared that anyone who disobeyed would be "cut off from Israel" (Ex. 12:15)."[72] If God's desire was to save the firstborn, the Passover had to be in the Genesis account as this firstborn from the dead is none other than Christ (Colossians 1:18) who was—destined before the foundation of the world (1 Peter 1:20).

Another significant point of the Passover is that along with the high-priestly role of Christ, is the adoption process of mankind by God. First Corinthians 6:19-20 tells the saints are not their own, they were bought with a price so as to help the saints understand their new state in Christ. Demonstrating that they are no longer slaves to the old written code of the law, but slaves to the new law of spirit (Romans 7:6; 8:12-17). Sin is synonymous with slavery. John 8:34 says *"most assuredly, I say to you, whoever commits sin is a slave to sin."* None is exempt from this form of slavery not even the descendant of Abraham. Beasley-Murray notes that "bondage to sin is a reality for every one who sins, including Abraham's children. Unlike slavery that is external, this is an inward condition from which one cannot flee, with its roots in a wrong relation to God. Such a slave needs a redeemer!"[73] It is the administration that changed with Christ emphasizing the spiritual intent of the law for mankind's freedom—a cause God has been instilling in humanity since creation. Mankind chose evil and is enslaved by its desire. Christ, however, did not give into the evil of the flesh when tempted because His desire was to do the will of the Father.

---

[72] Scott, B. 1997. *The Feasts of Israel* (electroniced.). The Friends of Israel Gospel Ministry, Inc.: Bellmawr, New Jersey

[73] Beasley-Murray, G. R. 2002. *Vol. 36: Word Biblical Commentary: John*. Word Biblical Commentary. Word, Incorporated: Dallas

In Romans 7:14 Paul declares, "the law is spiritual." Thus, the institution of the new symbols—bread and wine—was simply to "replace the need to slay a literal lamb every year, for the Messiah, the real Passover Lamb, has already been slain."[74] God requires a true heart before him. The true heart is one whose conscience has been cleansed from the dead works of sin to serve the true and living God. This cleansing of our conscience represents "freedom not only from sin and the damage sin has done, but also emancipation from the impairing left by sin from all the distortions left in mind and imagination."[75] It's a circumcision of the heart. God is seeking hearts that will obey Him, not only in the rituals and ceremonies performed but also from a conscience that is true. Read the details of the Priesthood and the slaying of the lamb. In the story of the Exodus it was roasted and eaten and the blood was spread across the doors and lintels while in the Levitical Priesthood it was the Priest's responsibility. "The doors and lintels signify that one accepts the promise of God to deliver the firstborn from death before the midnight cry which announces the taking away of the bride from the enemy."[76] Symbolically, when a believer partakes in this service it is a sign he is applying the blood of the Passover Lamb to his mind and heart, which represent the doors and lintels of the soul. It is a sign of faith that the believer seeks deliverance from death and an acknowledgement of the promise of God to deliver. It is also an indication that the fulfilment of the Passover is both continuous and futuristic.

---

[74]   www.http://biblicalholidays.com
[75]   Chambers. O. 1996, c1960. *The Philosophy of Sin: And other studies on the problem of man's moral life. Marshall, Morgan & Scott: Hants UK.*
[76]   www.http://biblicalholidays.com

Luke 22:15-16 states, "Then *he said to them, 'With fervent desire I have desired to eat this Passover with you before I suffer; for I say to you, I will no longer eat of it until it is fulfilled in the kingdom of God.* Note the phrase 'until it be fulfilled in the kingdom of God.' The Kingdom of God is not here now but speaks of a future coming. Thus, Christians are obligated to keep it in this present day until the Messiah puts in his appearance. It is a celebration of God in worship. In Matthew 26, Christ refers to His body and blood in the new covenant for the remission of sins. If mankind is to be transformed into the image of God then they will have to learn the spirit of 'passing over' the sins of their fellow brethren as Christ did and that begins by practicing—keeping both the physical and spiritual Passover. When God 'passed over' the sin of mankind He freed him from the bondage of physical and spiritual death by taking his place. Sin separated mankind from God the Eternal, held him captive and resulted in a need for him to be released from the stronghold of the enemy, which is death. Death will be swallowed up in victory when the corrupt nature shall put on incorruption (1 Corinthians 15:54). By Christ Passover sacrifice, mankind has been granted freedom and can now come again boldly before His Lord and Master (Hebrews 10: 19; 4:16; Ephesians 2:18) as he did when he was naked and unashamed. Christ made a way through the flesh; He was tempted like we are, yet He was without sin—Hebrews 4:14-15. Thus, the intimacy that Adam had with his Creator and Lord is now in the reconciliation process to be fulfilled at the second coming of God the Eternal—the marriage supper of the lamb.

While the official inauguration of the Passover occurred when God delivered a people called out of Egypt, another purpose was to give the universe a 'prophetic preview' of His awesome plan to 'pass over' and deliver His people at the appointed time. It was to make Himself known as the sovereign God and Lord of the universe. In Ezekiel 20:12, speaking of the Exodus experience the Lord said 'moreover I gave them My Sabbaths, to be a sign between them and Me, that they might know that I am the LORD who sanctifies them.' The sign of the people of God is the sign of the Sabbaths, not just the seventh day Sabbath but the annual Sabbaths proclaimed in the Annual Feast days. Observing the Sabbath meant to stand apart from those who did not confess Israel's faith—and to stand with God and his declared will. It was a distinctive sign of the covenant that God gave (Exodus 31:13-17).

Continuing, keep in mind that sin is about idolatry—the principal denial of God's providence to grant all that He has promised and mankind is prone to its power. Watson mentioned that we are prone "because we are led much by visible objects, and love to have our senses pleased."[77] Before the Exodus the children of Israel were steeped in idolatry. This evil proclivity disguises itself as something good in the form of leaven. As a result the Passover is not without unleavened bread, which Israel partook of in a hasty departure (Exodus 12). Leaven in scripture is symbolic of sin (pride), the evil that likes to exalt itself above God and others but Unleavened bread represents that which has no sin. Only the Messiah is described in the Bible as being without sin-without stain or spot. "*He had done no violence, nor was any deceit in His mouth*" (Isaiah. 53:9). In the New

---

[77]   Watson, T. 2000. *The Ten Commandments* (electroniced.). Ephesians Four Group: Escondito, California

Testament, we see the symbolism of leaven was magnified to represent hypocrisy (falsehood) (Matthew 23:25-28); false doctrines (Matthew 16: 2,12; Mark 8:15); greed and false zeal (Matthew 23:14-15); a misconception of spiritual values (Matthew 23:16-22); omission of justice and mercy (Matthew 23:23); formalistic obedience (Matthew 23:24); intolerance (Matthew 23:29-33); cruelty (Matthew 23:34-36) and malice (1Corinthians 5:7-8); all ignited by pride: the kind that puffs up and boasts so as to feel superior to others. It is the kind of spirit that is against truth and the will of God. All are the desires of the flesh (Galatians 5:16-21) and must be cleansed before one can become that new creature to reign with Christ in the Kingdom of God.

Israel was brought out of the land of Egypt in a roundabout manner so that the nations would see their deliverance and they, in turn, could be a light to the nations around them. However, Israel, according to Romans 9:32, did not pursue the law by faith. Their ignorant zeal was the source of their stumbling at believing in Christ and being that light to the nations who needed salvation. Greg Bahnsen writes that—

> "It was incredible pride and self-deception that caused the Jews to "rely on the law" and to be confident that they possessed "in the law the embodiment of knowledge" that made them self-righteous of others (Rom. 2:17-21), when in fact these who "brag about the law" were notoriously guilty of transgressing the law and dishonouring God."[78]

---

[78] Bahnsen. Greg L. (1996). In the book *Five Views on Law and Gospel.* Zondervan Publishing House. Grand Rapids,

This God whom Israel missed is none other than Jesus Christ the Messiah, the Lamb of God who takes away the sin of the world, our Unleavened Bread.(John 1:29)

The evil of leaven exhibited by Satan is also representative of Egypt or Babylon—a governmental system of worship that is built on the need to sustain and maintain power at all cost. Even to the point of mental and physical slavery to others. Recall that sin in the angelic realm and for mankind was not only "a spiritual offense against God . . . but also a governmental offense against Him as Ruler."[79] It is this restoration of government that Christ and the apostles preached—the Kingdom of God (Matthew 4:23; Mark. 1:14; Luke 4:43). It is the restoration of that which was in the Garden—without evil. This leaven of pride must be removed, hence, the cleansing of leaven from our physical homes and houses of our mind during the seven days. Unleavened Bread is the unblemished body of Christ. Jesus in Mark 14:22

> "When He had given thanks, He broke it [the unleavened bread], and said, Take, eat; this is my body, which is broken for you: this do in remembrance of me" (1 Cor. 11:24). The symbolism was clear. In Jewish teaching, leaven was representative of "the evil impulse of the heart." Jesus Himself applied the allegory to the pervasive, evil doctrine of the Pharisees, Sadducees, and Herod (Mt. 16:11; Mk. 8:15). In applying the symbol

---

Michigan. 94-95

[79] Strickland. Wayne G. (1996). In the book *Five Views on Law and Gospel.* Zondervan Publishing House. Grand Rapids, Michigan. 239

of the unleavened bread to His own body, Jesus was saying that His life contained no evil or sin."[80]

God wants to free humanity from this bondage created by the enemy in both a physical and spiritual manner because it causes death.

Mankind's liberation cannot be experienced through the workings of politics but through the supernatural and miraculous power of the Almighty God, which must not be taken for granted (Romans 6:1; 15). Nor should His freedom be thought of in the sense that the world uses freedom. Freedom as expressed by the world is that humanity is free to do whatever they so desire but this so-called demonstration of freedom impinges on the rights of others in a way that offends the Lord God of the universe. Moller in commenting on freedom notes,

> "Man either lives within the field of force radiated by the Spirit of God, or within that of the evil powers. It is impossible for man to belong solely to himself. Because he is of God, exists through God and has his destiny in God, his freedom is only possible in and with God and he can only find fulfilment in serving Him. Therefore, total submission to God in a disposition of love and obedience does not imply enslavement, but constitutes liberation and self-realisation."[81]

---

[80]   Scott. B. 1997. *The Feasts of Israel* (electronic ed.). The Friends of Israel Gospel Ministry, Inc.: Bellmawr, new Jersey.

[81]   Moller, F. P. 1998, c1997. *Vol. 3: From Sin to Salvation*. Words of light and life. Van Schaik Religious Books: Pretoria

In Exodus 8:1 *"thus says the Lord: 'Let my people go, that they may serve me.'* This means that God frees mankind to serve Him on His terms and should not be understood, as an occasion to satisfy our base desires (Galatians 5:13). Humanity's liberation must not be seen as merely physical as the need for both the physical and spiritual (mental) freedom must be addressed. This is so because the mind feeds on the desire for the physical; what it can see. It is to satisfy what we can see that starts us off the path to freedom and life and unto the path of death. Freedom is the capacity to express the true nature of the divine, the essence of the human soul through the spirit to which it was connected at the beginning. Sin starts in the mind of man therefore, the need for mental freedom is to be stressed over that of the physical. Paul in Romans 8:7 spoke of the carnal mind that is enmity against God. This mind rejects the dominion of God which "inevitably results in man being delivered to the evil forces that are active in him and in the world. Although God curtailed the activities of the evil forces, they are still so potent that they dominate and enslave man totally (Rom 6:12, 17; Hos 4:11)."[82] While both are of importance "spiritual slavery is much more bitter than mere physical slavery,"[83] and is not as easily perceived as that of the physical.

Look at Matthew 15:19-20 and James 1:14-15. Notice the defilement of man comes from the heart, which ignites our physical actions. "At the heart of the solicitation to evil . . . lies the personal desire that is bent on self-interest

---

[82]   Moller, F. P. 1998, c1997. *Vol. 3: From Sin to Salvation*. Words of light and life. Van Schaik Religious Books: Pretoria

[83]   Scott. B. 1997. *The Feasts of Israel* (electroniced.). The Friends of Israel Gospel Ministry, Inc.: Bellmawr, new Jersey.

and self-pleasing."[84] It is in celebrating the Feast of God that obedience and honour is shown for what He has done. The Saints celebrate the Feast with a heart of love as it comes around yearly, and this is well pleasing in the sight of God. This love of God was demonstrated through Jesus Christ who did not seek to please Himself but to do the will of the Father. Likewise, mankind's freedom is demonstrated in him pleasing the Almighty God as Christ did. It is all good and well that we are free physically but if still bound up in sin within the consciousness of our minds, we are still in bondage. This was seen in the Pharisees whom Jesus Christ taught His disciples to beware of. They were enslaved to the rituals and ceremonies but forgot the weightier matters of the law (Matthew 23). They could not see God in Christ because of their flawed focus. However, Christ did not negate the physical but emphasised both when He said; these you ought to have done without leaving the others undone.' In Romans 12:1, Paul emphasizes the need to be transformed by the renewing of our minds and as a result, mankind must continue to battle the lust and need for power—the Adamic nature. This can only occur when mankind, out of love for God choose to exit the Egypt of their lives on both levels to worship the true God of heaven. Moller avows, "the application of Christ's victory over sin in our lives begins with a change of heart, also called rebirth. That is when we receive the spirit of Christ, and his life becomes our life."[85]

---

[84] Martin. R. P. 2002. *Vol. 48: Word Biblical Commentary: James*. Word Biblical Commentary. Word, Incorporated: Dallas.

[85] Moller, F. P. 1998, c1997. *Vol. 3: From Sin to Salvation*. Words of light and life. Van Schaik Religious Books: Pretoria

Like the children of Israel who looked to politics for deliverance so do all peoples since Adam including those of the New Testament. Notice in John 12 that the people were not looking for a spiritual saviour but a political one. The liberating God is both. The Gospel or Good News is about the Kingdom of God which is in relation to the restoration of a literal government here on earth; the one that was broken because of sin. It was what Christ, the prophets and apostles preached (Matthew 4:23; Mark 1:14; Luke 4:43) and is both a spiritual and physical kingdom. Mankind today, constantly look to the political governments of this world to save them but no such rescue is forthcoming. Egypt represents the sin-laden world of Satan in all its glory and was a nation with military and economic strength and Israel was enslaved by her patronage and power. Ryken etal point out that "Egypt is a symbol that embodies the political and military temptation to turn to idolatrous superpowers instead of to Yahweh in times of acute crisis."[86] The liberation would come through witnessing the final downfall of Egypt's power that was used to make an indelible mark on the minds of the children of Israel was always looking to Egypt for rescue but as Isaiah noted, "Egypt's shade cannot provide protection, but only shame and defeat (Is. 30:1-5; cf. 20:1-6; 31:1-7)."[87] God had to destroy the nation so they would not return to it. He does not want us to return to sin but to Him, and to stand firm in the liberty with which we were freed (Galatians 5:1). Again, sin was a spiritual offence against God and also a governmental offence against Him as ruler. Israel's

---

[86] Ryken, L., Wilhoit, J., Longman, T., Duriez, C., Penney, D., & Reid, D. G. 2000, c 1998. *Dictionary of Biblical Imagery* (electronic ed.). InterVarsity Press: Downers Grove, IL.

[87] ibid

deliverance was not designed to only restore that broken relationship of fellowship but also to restore harmony with the governmental authority of the universe. The ruler of this coming government who will stand as King of kings and Lord of lords at the coming of the eternal Kingdom of God is none other than Jesus the Christ.

Unlike Satan and the first Adam, who in pride exalted their positions, Christ did not hold on to power (Philippians 2:5-8) or desire it for Himself. He had it and gave it up in order to share it with His woman (The Church) and children—the heirs of salvation. That's what love is (love is sharing power) and love needs to be expressed; which Christ demonstrated on the cross. Philippians 2:5-8 speaks about how Christ emptied himself of his divinity "Let *this mind be in you which was also in Christ Jesus, who, being in the form of God, did not consider it robbery to be equal with God, but made Himself of no reputation, taking the form of a bondservant, and coming in the likeness of men. And being found in appearance as a man, He humbled Himself and became obedient to point of death, even the death of the cross.*" Love frees one to do the will of God as Christ did; it has no fear of loss. Adam feared losing his position as head which he did because of not submitting to the Father. R. P. Martin commented that

"As the first Adam was in the image and likeness of God (Gen 1:26-27), so Christ, the second Adam, existed in the image of God (Phil 2:6). Whereas the first Adam wrongly tried to become like God (Gen 3:5), the second Adam either did not strive to be equal with God or did not regard equality with God as a thing to be retained."[88]

As was noted, it was the administration of the law that changed and some new symbols were instituted; namely—bread and wine along with the washing of feet. These new symbols are lessons in humility and the power of love, for God and fellow brethren and also symbolic of Christ's blood and body. We see in the New Testament where Christ, in demonstrating his love for His disciples and humanity took on the form of a servant by washing their feet and encouraging them to act in like manner (John 13:5-17). The message of the washing of feet is **not** a "putting up with sin" as is sometimes promoted in some church circles. God never puts up with sin! If one is 'putting up with' there is no need to wash because washing means a cleansing away of dirt. Bruce Scott in his commentary notes that,

> "The object lesson was clear: Not only was Jesus exemplifying the epitome of servanthood, He was also demonstrating a spiritual principle that He had taught many times before. Outward washings are merely symbols of what should be true on the inside; inward, spiritual cleanliness takes precedence over that which is outward."[89]

---

[88] Martin. R. P. 2004. *Vol. 43: Word Biblical Commentary: Philippians.* Word Biblical Commentary. Word, Incorporated: Dallas.

[89] Scott. B. 1997. *The Feasts of Israel* (electronic ed.). The Friends of Israel Gospel Ministry, Inc.: Bellmawr, new Jersey.

God's desire is that we learn that it is *'not what goes into the mouth that defiles a man; but what comes out of the mouth, this defiles a man . . . but those things which proceed out of the mouth come from the heart, and they defile a man. For out of the heart proceed evil thoughts, murders, adulteries, fornications, thefts, false witness, and blasphemies. These are the things which defile a man, but to eat with unwashed hands does not defile a man,'* (Matthew 15: 11-20). Judas' life so ably displays that one can actually be participating in the work and rituals, yet have an evil and unrepentant heart. God was willing to cleanse Judas. He, however, was not willing to be cleansed but hardened his heart to feed his own desire. When mankind fails to accept the cleansing of God in the person and work of Jesus Christ, he ends up killing himself—physically and spiritually. God's desire is that his saints will "assist in" the cleansing of the sin of their brother or sister by killing the egotistic (prideful) nature and perform the 'menial' task of washing someone else's feet, not out of mere ritual but as done from a true heart.

Washing of feet was considered a menial task as it was performed by the servants to a visitor to the house, as an aspect of hospitality. However, Christ has elevated the servant's status to that of friends (John 15:15) and ministers of His. God is asking that as He washed and cleansed our sins by calling us and making the truth known to us, we are to act in like manner. Not that we are in the position of God the Eternal, but as ambassadors of His (2 Corinthians 5:20), he has declared mankind 'gods' (Psalm 82:6; John 10:35), to be His representatives here on earth until He returns and transforms our lowly bodies to that of His. Examine John 13:5-17 Christ knew that Peter, who initially did not want to be washed, was going to deny Him.

However, Christ made provision for his betrayal, by His grace, to have him restored after his open denial of Him. To love as Christ or to reproduce the character of God, one will have to forgive as He did. He said "For *I have given you an example, that you should do as I have done to you.*" (v15) Love must be expressed in our actions of faith. It's our Passover. Once Christ, the Passover Lamb, extended grace to Peter He commanded that he showed that love to others. Note in Luke 22:32 where Christ said when you have turned again strengthen your brethren. All of humanity is called to the task of "passing over" the sin of our brethren in like manner as Christ did—the act of love. The saints are each assigned the task of cleansing each other's feet so that they may all be considered worthy to enter the house of God. It is laid down in the Ten Commandments, which were explained by the ordinances and judgements. Christ said "*by this all will know that you are my disciples, if you have love for one another*" (John 13:35). Christ loves us as His very own self and thus the command to love thy neighbour as thyself (Romans 13:9; Galatians 5:14). It is this love which we have for God, and by extension for our fellow brethren, that opens the door of faith (1 John 4: 7-21) to the eternal Passover at the coming Kingdom of God—the future Messianic Banquet (Mark 14:25; Matthew 26:29; Luke 22: 16, 18).

Another symbolic feature to mention as it pertains to feet is that the feet are also figures of authority over a person or place. The ordinary "feet are not normally considered attractive and may be thought of as inferior (1 Cor. 12: 15, 21)." The right to own or lose property was also determined by the feet that touched or did not walk on (Deuteronomy

2:5; 11:24; Joshua 1:3; Psalm 122:2; 2 Chronicles 33:8). [90] Christ, the Passover Lamb, as pictured in the New Testament, has authority over all things by subjecting them under His feet (Matthew 22:44; 1 Corinthians 15:25ff.; Ephesians 1:22; Hebrews 2:8); and the eventual victory of Christian believers over Satan and his followers (Isaiah 49:23; 60: 14; Romans 16:20; Revelation 3:9). Christ has the authority to cleanse the feet of those considered unworthy making them worthy to enter the Kingdom of God. It is the washing of feet that gives authority to believers to carry out the commission in Matthew 28:18. Note Christ's response again to Peter in John 13. In verse 8, Jesus answering Peter said, "*if I do not wash you, you have no part with Me.*" The washing cleanses us so that we can have communion with God. Christ, our elder brother, chose the role of a servant to accomplish this mission. His aim is to teach us that we are not to live as Cain who killed his brother (Genesis 4:9; 1 John 3:12) but to show that we are our brother's keeper. This washing of feet also teaches that none of us is above the other; all are on the same playing field when it comes to sin. However, this is not an instance to do away with church government because Jesus Christ himself acknowledged (John 13:16) that a servant is not greater than his master who washes his feet. This is a preview of the saint's soon-to-be-fulfilled destiny as Spirit-beings.

Let us consider the wedding banquet as it may help us solve the mystery surrounding the public reading of the Song of Songs as part of the Jewish tradition at the Passover

---

[90]   Ryken, L., Wilhoit, J., Longman, T., Duriez, C., Penney, D., & Reid, D. G. 2000, c 1998. *Dictionary of Biblical Imagery* (electronic ed.). InterVarsity Press: Downers Grove, IL.

celebration. The book is considered the Holy of the holies but frowned upon by some claim to be "church fathers" who felt the book should not even be read due to its sexual content. One famous Jewish Rabbi, Akiba, claimed that, "the whole world is not worth the day on which the Song of Songs was given to Israel; for all the Scriptures are holy, but the Song of Songs is the Holy of Holies."[91] The book praises the human body—all of it: the cheeks (1:10), eyes (1:15), hair (6:5), teeth, neck and breast (4:2, 4-5) and again the feet (7:1). All of which is believed to have played a vital role in the service of God and Israel's redemption from Egypt. According to Jewish history, the feet are "praised because of their part in allowing a person to make the pilgrimage to Jerusalem for . . . the festivals."[92] As Jesus was preparing to be crucified, his feet were anointed (Luke 7:38) with perfumed oil by a woman who felt His love and in return expressed her love to him the best way she knew how. Ephesians 6:15 asks that the saints "*shod their feet with the preparation of the Gospel of peace;*" that is be in readiness, with the Gospel of Peace like Christ did in obedience to the Father.

The Song of Songs helps us to realize that all are made in the image and likeness of God and, therefore, each component is part of His holy image and plays a vital function in the operation of the body. In 1 Corinthians 12:21, Paul emphasized the importance of all parts of the body; "*and the eye cannot say to the hand, "I have no need of you"; nor again the head to the feet, "I have no need of you."*

---

[91] Davidson, R. M. A. 2001, c 1986. *Ecclesiastes and the Song of Solomon.* The Daily Study Series. Westminster John Knox Press: Louisville.

[92] www.torah.org/learning/yomtov/pesach/5758/vol4no03.html(2008)

All make up the human frame and each part is critical to the effective functioning of the body. The body also shows the intimacy of the relationship with which God desires of His people. Though each member acts differently they are all connected to the purpose of God. The woman Christ adores and will marry is the church who is intimately involved in obeying His will and so must each member of the body be adored.

It is acknowledged that God is Spirit and, therefore, any reference to God's body is simply a figure of speech; a means of making God's actions more comprehensible. However, in scripture God is described as having hands (Deuteronomy 5:15) and feet (Exodus 24:10) indicating the close relationship between the physical and the spiritual. "With each good deed done by an organ or limb (*member of the body*), the splendour of creation and the holiness of God is evident;"[93] so it is with the members of the church. When the human body is used for the service of God, we are ensuring that our bodies, the images of God in us, are acting as the conduits of holiness as they should. This is why Paul could admonish the brethren in Romans 12:1, "*I beseech you therefore, brethren, by the mercies of God, that you present your bodies a living sacrifice, holy, acceptable to God, which is your reasonable service.*" Christ presented His whole body in service and sacrifice and never once gave into its desires even when tempted after forty days of fasting (Matthew 4). The body should not be used in dishonour and Paul again admonished those in Corinth (1 Corinthians 5) when he found that there was sexual immorality among

---

[93]   www.torah.org/learning/yomtov/pesach/5758/vol4no03. html

them—a kind he said that is not named among the pagans. He asked that such a person be delivered to Satan so that the soul (the consciousness of man) may be saved in the day of the Lord.

The good that God wants to see in humanity is something that each and every person has the innate ability to attain at the highest degree. Because mankind is created in God's image, we have a tremendous responsibility in assuming that this image does not become sullied or tarnished. When we act in accordance to the will of God with every limb, we become a manifestation of God's holiness, a temple in which He delights to dwell.

While the children of Israel were in Egypt, Pharaoh wanted to destroy the intimacy of family relationships by having the men working harder and not going home to their wives. (God is about family relationships and intimacy) However, the women sensed the plan of the enemy which was to destroy the family (so that the nation of Israel could not grow) and being more proactive, acted in faith, by taking intimacy to the work site by taking the men fish and water and "had marital relations with them among the sheep folds."[94] God wants His woman (the church) to be in close relationship with Him despite the threat of the enemy. He promised that He would never leave nor forsake her. In the same way that the women used their bodies to create the intimacy that Pharaoh tried to kill, God desires that intimacy of the Church of God today. Paul said of the body in Romans 12:4-5 "*For as we have many members in*

---

[94]   www.torah.org/learning/yomtov/pesach/5761/vol7no01. html.

one body, but all the members do not have the same function, so we, being many, are one body in Christ, and individually, members of one another." There are some who deem that other parts of the body is sick while other parts remain whole but forget that the body with its many members is fitly joined together for the fulfilling of the purpose of God (1 Corinthians 12:12, 27; Ephesians 4:12, 16). Thus, the Song of Songs is seen as the book, which celebrates the woman's (Israel's/church's) freedom—free from physical and spiritual bondage; to reproduce and bear godly children. It is because of the dual aspect of freedom that the human body is praised; "something very physical, something that we often remove from the realm of the spiritual."[95] The Passover serves as the model lifestyle of the child of God because Jesus as the Passover Lamb is constantly making intercession for those whom He loves and died for. It is also through the body (physical) that we are asked to do this just as Christ did.

---

[95] www.torah.org/learning/yomtov/pesach/5758/vol4no03.html

Pentecost

Jesus Christ is our Firstfruit and our Wavesheaf Offering

According Samuele Bacchiocchi "the Passover could not be observed until at least some of the barley was ready for harvest."[96] This spring harvest was known as the feast of the first fruits, which began on the day after the Sabbath (Leviticus 23: 11, 15). The day was referred to as the first day of Unleavened Bread and was also considered a Sabbath. Bruce Scott notes

> "The Feast of Weeks (Ex. 34:22) is also known in Scripture by other names. It is referred to as the "feast of harvest" (Ex. 23:16) because it inaugurated the beginning of the wheat harvest. It is called the "day of the first fruits" (Num. 28:26) because its primary purpose was to bring a designated portion of the harvest, the "first fruits," into the Temple as an act of dedication to God in recognition of His provision. The festival is also termed in the New Testament as "Pentecost" (lit., *fiftieth*) [Acts 2:1], signifying the *fiftieth* day from the waving of the *omer* (*sheaf*) of first fruits (Lev. 23:15-16)."[97]

There are two sets of harvest—barley or omer and wheat. The barley was offered during the Passover Week

---

[96]   Bacchiocchi, Samuele. (1995). *God's Festivals in Scripture and History: Part 1 The Spring Festivals.* Biblical Perspectives. Berrien Springs, Michigan. 167

[97]   Scott, Bruce. 1997. *The Feasts of Israel* (electronic ed.). The Friends of Israel Gospel Ministry, Inc.: Bellmawr, New Jersey

(Leviticus 23:10-14) while the first fruit of the wheat harvest was offered on the fiftieth day following the barley harvest (Exodus 34:22; Leviticus 23:17). Barley and wheat are both grains used in the making of bread but barley is of a higher quality and has far more nutritional value than wheat. Barley was harvested around the time of the Passover while wheat was harvested seven weeks later at the Feast of the First Fruit/Weeks which came to be known as the Feast of Pentecost in the New Testament. "The reaping was so important that it could be done even on the Sabbath,"[98] and was watched over by temple officials who had their own basket and sickle for reaping.

The offering of the early first fruits/barley sheaf took place after the day of the Passover. On this day the wave-sheaf offering of the first fruit/barley was waved before the Lord for acceptance. Leviticus 23:10-14 reads *"Speak to the people of Israel, and say to them: when you come into the land which I give to you and reap its harvest, then you shall bring a sheaf of the first-fruits of your harvest to the priest. He shall wave the sheaf before the Lord, to be accepted; on your behalf; on the day after the Sabbath the priest shall wave it. And you shall offer on that day, when you wave the sheaf, a male lamb a year of the first year, without blemish, as a burnt offering to the Lord . . . You shall eat neither bread nor parched grain nor fresh grain until this same day that you have brought an offering to your God; it shall be a statue forever throughout your generations in all your dwellings."* This wave sheaf was none other than Jesus Christ who was accepted by the Father as the perfect sacrifice for sins, John 20:11-18.

---

[98]   Scott, Bruce. 1997. *The Feasts of Israel* (electronic ed.). The Friends of Israel Gospel Ministry, Inc.: Bellmawr, New Jersey

Pentecost was a pilgrimage festival that saw the children of Israel being accepted by God as a people and nation. The acceptance of the sacrifices Israel made while in Egypt was an indication that they were ready to accept Yahweh as Lord and forsake the idolatry of the land to which they were enslaved. This was to fulfil the promise He had made to Abraham (Genesis 12. 1-3) and to show how Abraham himself forsook the land of Ur (Genesis 11:27-28, 31; 15:7; Nehemiah 9:7) in which he too was in idolatry. The Spirit of truth descended on the nation empowering them to keep the law of God (love in the spirit in which it was given) which was codified on tablets of stone at Mount Sinai. God chose to set Israel apart and in this way and gave the Ten Commandments with loud claps of thunder so that all the nations around them could hear and know that obedience to the law was what was demanded of anyone who would follow the God of Israel. In His sovereignty, God allowed the other nations to hear so that they would come and worship the true and living God, with Israel being a light unto them. Because of pride and self-deception (Romans 2: 17-21) they relied on the physical aspects of the law, fell prey to the avenue they themselves were trying to rid themselves of and time after time sat in the seat of idolatry.

If sin is about idolatry, let's examine how the codified law in the form of the Ten Commandments is reflected in these commands of God. God had delivered them from idolatry and was giving them His commandments that would allow them to forsake that lifestyle, along with the nations around them who were also idolaters. Now, according to James 2: 8-10; Galatians 5:3 and Matthew 5:19, the law of God is viewed as a single unit and contains the Gospel (Hebrews 3:16-18; 4:2). Therefore, exploring them has impact for the world, for which Christ died and for those called in obedience. The injunction of God given in Exodus 20 is basically divided into two but the unity of it still stands and has its foundation in the love of God. In Matthew 22:39; Romans 13:8-10; Galatians 5:7-14 the word of God declares that **all** aspects of the law are summed up in loving God first and thy neighbour as thyself; two dimensions of the whole. Christ practiced this and taught it as the means to inherit Eternal Life (Luke 10:27-28). Remember that sin is anything that goes against God and man who will be clothed with the glory of divinity. If the character of God is love and mankind is here to imitate and reflect that divine image, the test of obedience is required and he will have to pass the same test Jesus did. The Ten Commandments deal with how mankind must express their love for God and for their neighbour. The first four injunctions are centred around God while the following six are around humanity. Let's begin this synopsis.

(1) In Exodus 20: 3 we see "*You shall have no other gods before me.* Not that there are any other gods (1 Corinthians 8:5) but God demands that nothing in life be placed before Him. 'They are called such not because they are so, either by nature or by office (Psa. 82:6), but because the corrupt hearts of men make and esteem them such—as in "whose god is their belly." (Phil. 3:19). [99] Any decision, tradition of worship (Matthew 15:9; Acts 14:15); that goes before God's desired will is considered idolatry and amounts to nothing. Pink notes that

---

[99]   Pink, A. W. 2000. *The Ten Commandments* (electronic ed.). Ephesians Four Group: Escondido, CA

"this Commandment *sees* willful ignorance of God and His will through despising those means by which we may acquaint ourselves with Him (*Rom. 1:20-21*); . . . . atheism or the denial of God; . . . . the setting up of false and fictitious gods; . . . disobedience and self-will or the open defiance of God; and . . . , all inordinate and immoderate affections or the setting of our hearts and minds upon other objects. They are idolaters and transgressors of this first commandment who manufacture a "God" as a figment of their own minds."[100]

(2) V. 4-6—*You shall not make for yourself a carved image—any likeness of anything that is in heaven above, or that is in the earth beneath, or that is in the water under the earth; you shall not bow down to them nor serve them. For I, the LORD your God, am a jealous God, visiting the iniquity of the fathers upon the children to the third and fourth generations of those who hate Me, but showing mercy to thousands, to those who love Me and keep My commandments.* "God is incorporeal, invisible, and can be realized only by a **spiritual** principle;[101] John 4:24 declares God is Spirit and has no semblance of anything, therefore, making any image of Him in worship amounts to idolatry. Thomas Watson, in the book the **Ten Commandments** alerts us to the fact that 'it is idolatry, not only to worship a false god, but the true God in a false manner."[102]

---

[100] Ibid

[101] Ibid

[102] Watson, T. 2000. *The Ten Commandments* (electronic ed.). Ephesians Four Group: Escondito, California

(3) V. 7—*You shall not take the name of the LORD your God in vain, for the LORD will not hold him guiltless who takes His name in vain.* God has a purpose for what he does, therefore, taking the Lord's name (making a vow)in vain is termed as swearing because mankind cannot create what God has created (Matthew 5:33-37 Leviticus 19:12). The name of God must be held in reverence (Deuteronomy 28:58). It is idolatry that sees mankind belittling the name of God to suit their desires for belief and trust. Pink points out that

> "this Commandment prohibits all dishonoring thoughts of God, all needless, flippant, profane, or blasphemous mention of Him, any irreverent use of His Word, any murmurings against His providence, any abuse of anything by which He has made Himself known."[103]

(4) V. 8-11—*Remember the Sabbath day, to keep it holy. Six days you shall labor and do all your work, but the seventh day is the Sabbath of the LORD your God. In it you shall do no work: you, nor your son, nor your daughter, nor your male servant, nor your female servant, nor your cattle, nor your stranger who is within your gates. For in six days the LORD made the heavens and the earth, the sea, and all that is in them, and rested the seventh day. Therefore the LORD blessed the Sabbath day and hallowed it.* God has declared the Sabbath a day of rest because He knows what's best for man not the other way around. "Worshipping on the first day of the week is not what

---

[103] Pink, A. W. 2000. *The Ten Commandments* (electronic ed.). Ephesians Four Group: Escondido, CA

the fourth commandment requires: it explicitly requires cessation of work on the seventh day."[104] It is idolatry to think we can choose a day of worship and rest because it is easy and convenient and that God will understand or, better yet, that the God of yesterday, today and forever, who changes not will change the law to suit rebellious mankind. God would not make a command of mankind that He knew they could not keep. He demands obedience as a way of showing love for Him. The Sabbath is the day of the Lord. Mankind cannot choose which day they deem important and therefore, have idolized their desire above that of God.

(5) V. 12—*Honor your father and your mother, that your days may be long upon the land which the* LORD *your God is giving you.* "This commandment to honor parents is much broader in its scope than appears at first glance. It is not to be restricted to our literal **father** and **mother**, but is to be applied to all our superiors."[105] Adam and Eve disobeyed their first parent; forsaking the wisdom of the God to seek their own. As the relationship with Yahweh is the beginning of the covenant so it should be with the human family. Children are to honour their parents in the fear of the Lord (Matthew 19: 27-30); forsaking parental guidance is seen as disobeying Yahweh and can be labelled idolatry.

---

[104] Moo. Douglas J (1996). In the book *Five Views on Law and Gospel.* Zondervan Publishing House. Grand Rapids, Michigan. 88

[105] Pink, A. W. 2000. *The Ten Commandments* (electronic ed.). Ephesians Four Group: Escondido, CA 38

(6) V. 13—*You shall not murder.* Adam became angry and blamed God for putting temptation in his way though he made the choice to disobey the command given him. His anger was "Unadvised anger. Anger boils in the veins, and often produces murder."[106] He wished she had not existed at that time, not knowing he was elevating his own importance and status as first created. Also because they were both one in flesh his condemnation of her saw his own death. Read the story of Cain and Abel in Genesis 4. Genesis 9:6 states that man was made in the image of God and, therefore, anyone who sheds the blood of another shall have his blood shed too. Ezekiel 22:3-4 and 2 Kings 3:27 connect murder with idolatry; it is the character trait of the enemy (John 8:44). Pink points out that,

> "This commandment is not restricted to forbidding the actual crime of murder. It also prohibits all the degrees and causes of murder, such as rash anger and hatred, slanders and revenge, and whatever else may prejudice the safety of our neighbor or tempt us to see him perish when it is in our power to relieve and rescue him."[107]

Not all killing was considered murder, as accidental slaying was not deemed chargeable (Deuteronomy 19:5);

(7) V. 14—*You shall not commit adultery.* Adultery is being unfaithful to one's partner. The Hebrew word is *na aph*

---

[106] Watson, T. 2000. *The Ten Commandments* (electronic ed.). Ephesians Four Group: Escondido, California

[107] Pink, A. W. 2000. *The Ten Commandments* (electronic ed.). Ephesians Four Group: Escondido, CA 42

[naw-af] and means to apostatize. Israel was unfaithful to God by playing the harlot after other gods and so did Adam and Eve. They were unfaithful to the God of their salvation, becoming selfish in their deeds to satisfy themselves. Christ magnified this command in the New Testament by showing that when one lusts after a woman one commits adultery (Matthew 5:28). That desire is selfish and idolatrous. It is coveting thy neighbour's property. "Adultery is not only a sin against the nation, it's a sin against the race of mankind, because each of us has a part in either developing or destroying the race of which we are a part."[108] In relationships, when a person indulges or encourages anyone to participate in the sin of adultery, he/she has become as selfish as Satan, seeking to gratify his/her own desires instead of following the will of God.

(8) V. 15 *You shall not steal.* Stealing always begins with covetousness and, therefore, leads to idolatry (Colossians 3:5). "The root from which theft proceeds is **discontent** with the portion God has allotted, and therefrom a coveting of what He has withheld from us and bestowed upon others."[109] It is the belief that what a person has must be yours without working for it. It is greed and indicates that one is not satisfied with what God has blessed him/her with.

---

[108] McGee, J. V. 2001, c1995. *Love, Liberation & the Law: The Ten Commandments* (electronic ed.). Thomas Nelson Publishers: Nashville

[109] Pink, A. W. 2000. *The Ten Commandments* (electronic ed.). Ephesians Four Group: Escondido, CA 52

(9) V. 16 *You shall not bear false witness against your neighbor.* Satan was the first to bear false witness against the Eternal. False witness has to do with slander and includes gossip (Proverbs 6:16, 19; Exodus 23:1) as it paints a negative picture of another person who is made in the image and likeness of God. Slandering "is to report things of others unjustly."[110] Those who participate elevate themselves above the other person in order to seek self-glory and gratification amounting to idolatry.

(10) *You shall not covet your neighbor's house; you shall not covet your neighbor's wife, or his male servant, or his female servant, or his ox, or his donkey, or anything that is your neighbor's.* "Covetousness is termed the secret sin; it 'is a sin that can't be discerned very easily. A person can covet and not be discovered,"[111] because it's conceived in the mind. Satan coveted the position of God and what He has in store for humanity—immortality. Covetousness is idolatry (Colossians 3:5) and should not be part of the life of the child of God. This commandment sums up the whole.

It is no wonder that Christ said 'Love is the fulfilling of the law and its codified message is planted in keeping the Ten Commandments. Thus, Jesus declares in John 14:15 *"if you love me keep my commandments,"* (1 John 5:3). It is through these commands that God teaches His love to

---

[110] Watson, T. 2000. *The Ten Commandments* (electronic ed.). Ephesians Four Group: Escondito, California

[111] McGee, J. V. 2001, c1995. Love, Liberation & the Law: The Ten Commandments (electronic ed.). Thomas Nelson Publishers: Nashville

humanity. Revelation 12:17 and 14:12 closes with the theme of obedience. It is those who keep the commandments of God and the testimony of Jesus Christ that will be saved. The demands of His law require a love for God that can only be done with the aid of God's Holy Spirit imprinted on the mind and heart of each individual. It was at Pentecost that this mark of identity was delivered to the nation of Israel as they journeyed to the Promised Land.

The harvesting of souls is also significant to Pentecost. Though all came out of Egypt, the test of true obedience was carried out at Mount Sinai through these very same commandments given to Moses. Exodus 20:20-21 reads: *And Moses said to the people, "Do not fear; for God has come to test you, and that His fear may be before you, so that you may not sin." So the people stood afar off, but Moses drew near the thick darkness where God was.* The people did not want to be intimate with God and this was illustrated by their withdrawal. It is those who do His will, will choose to draw close to His commands. God uses the sharp sickle of His word to cut off or draw close to Him, those in need of pruning (John 15) for his glory. A sickle is a sharp instrument that was used for harvesting by the priest and is used in scripture both literally and figuratively and "metaphorically as a tool of the harvest of human life at the Last Judgment (Rev. 14:14-20)".[112] The figurative use of the sickle is of God reaping the harvest that is ready. In Revelation 14: 14-19, the reaping of those who have kept the commandments of God is being administered. Then I

---

[112] Achtemeier, P. J., Harper & Row, P., & Society of Biblical Literature. 1985. Harper's Bible Dictionary. Includes index. (1st ed.). Harper & Row: San Francisco

looked, and behold, a white cloud, and on the cloud sat One like the Son of Man, having on his head a golden crown, and in his hand sharp sickle. And another angel came out from the temple, crying with a loud voice to him who sat on the cloud, "Thrust in Your sickle and reap, for the time has come for You to reap, for the harvest of the earth is ripe. So He who sat on the cloud thrust in His sickle upon the earth, and the earth was reaped. Then another angel came out of the temple, which is in heaven, he also having a sharp sickle. And another angel came out from the altar, who had power over fire, and he cried with a loud cry to him who had the sharp sickle, saying, *"Thrust in your sharp sickle and gather the clusters of the vine of the earth, for her grapes are fully ripe." So the angel thrust his sickle into the earth and gathered the vine of the earth, and threw it into the great winepress of the wrath of God. The sharpness of the 'sickle indicates that judgment is in view;*'[113] it is the Word of God that is able to pierce through the soul (Luke 2:35); which Christ will use to strike the nations at his coming (Revelation 19:15). As the wrath of God was poured out on those who left Egypt and still continue because of the sins of Babylon so it will be at the coming of the Kingdom of God.

For the people who left Egypt, it was a time to recount their pilgrimage from the Passover deliverance so that they could encounter with the God of liberation at Mount Sinai. It was a journey from physical liberation to spiritual redemption as freedom is on both levels. Samuele Bacchiocchi notes that the Jews "by counting forty nine

---

[113] Aune, D. E. 2002. Vol. 52B: Word Biblical Commentary: Revelation 6-16. Word Biblical Commentary . Word, Incorporated: Dallas

days between Passover and Pentecost declares that man does not attain complete freedom through physical liberation alone."[114] God wanted intimacy with His people, a desire he had from the beginning with Adam and Eve and thus commanded Moses to declare to Pharaoh *"Let my people go so that they might worship me"* (Exodus 5:1; 8:1). The Exodus experience was incomplete without Israel's acceptance of the law (love) of God on a spiritual level. It is a common notion taught by many that Israel did not have God's Holy Spirit and, proved, their failure to carry out His will by not keeping the law. Acts 7:51 disprove such claim. It reads—"You stiff-necked and uncircumcised in heart and ears! You always resist the Holy Spirit; as your fathers did, so do you." It is the spirit of the commandments that God wants us to live by and not the letter of it. The Spirit of God is His Word; His commands, in the form of the Ten Commandments, the truth through which the saints are sanctified. (John 17:17) Christ has simply placed it upon the hearts of the believer (Jeremiah 31:31-34) instead of tablets of stone. In a prophecy to Jeremiah, God declared that he would put His laws in the hearts of the people (Jeremiah 31:33; Heb. 8:10). Thus, the confirmation that the law was not new nor was it the problem—the problem was with the people. "The quality of newness intrinsic to the new covenant consists in the new manner of presenting God's law and not in newness of content."[115]

---

[114] Bacchiocchi. Samuele (1995). God's Festivals in Scripture and History: Part 1 The Spring Festivals. Biblical Perspectives. Berrien Springs, Michigan 179

[115] Lane, W. L. 2002. Vol. 47A: Word Biblical Commentary: Hebrews 1-8. Word Biblical Commentary. Word, Incorporated: Dallas

This new covenant was established to confirm mankind's redeemed hearts in obedience to God's law (Romans 8:4-10; 2 Corinthians 3:6-11) on a spiritual level. The conception that they didn't have the Spirit of God suggests that they did not have the inclination to keep the Law of God, which scripture denies. According to Deuteronomy 30:11-16 the commandments, statutes and judgements preceded from God are enveloped in loving thy neighbour as thyself and was not too mysterious for them to keep and these speak to the spiritual dimension, clearly in view. Why would God send Israel into captivity if they didn't have the inclination to keep the Law? They had the law but failed to keep it in the Spirit in which it was given. The idea would suggest that there is a different standard for Jews than that of Gentiles. The standard of God is same from the beginning until now and will be in the future (Hebrews 13:8).

Bacchiocchi in quoting from the Midrash makes the point "that when God gave the Torah on Sinai, His thundering voice reverberated in seventy languages so that all the nations should understand."[116] When the commandments were given, it was the Spirit of God that spoke and these spoken words were as fire burning into tablets of stone and all the nations around, including Israel was able to witness this event. These words, which were spoken and burnt into stone, were as if they were individually burnt into the hearts/souls of the people who witnessed the event to which all Israel agreed. It was the character—the love of God for all humanity that was being spoken through these Ten Commandments and the message of the Gospel that

---

[116] Bacchiocchi, Samule (1995). God's Festivals in Scripture and History. Biblical Perspectives. Berrien Spring, Michigan 178

was preached by Peter in Acts 2. Like the child of God in the present age, acceptance without the spirit is incomplete. Christ told his disciples in John 14 that He had to go to the Father so that they could be endowed with the comforting power of God's Holy Spirit. The Spirit of God helps the believer to overcome sin, guides and leads him/her into all truth (John 16: 13), thereby empowering the child of God to do the same works as Christ did and even greater because of His acceptance by the Father (John 14:12).

As we continue, keep in mind that the wave-sheaf offering and acceptance occurred during the Passover season while the children of Israel were on their way out of Egypt and the people were commanded to give thanks (Deuteronomy 26: 5, 8, 9, 10) for deliverance. They were also given instructions on how to celebrate the other annual festivals (Exodus 23: 10-19) that would become part of their sojourn. Ezekiel 20: 12, 20 confirm that these Feasts/ Sabbaths were given that the children of God may know that Yahweh was the Lord God and He sanctifies. Sanctification means to set apart. Israel was sanctified because of God's love and mercy, not their works. It is through keeping these feasts that mankind will come to know the true and loving God—not the pagan practices that seem to establish the traditions of men. Also of note was the fact that there was no agricultural harvest because the children of Israel were not in their physical land, therefore, God used the harvest of the nation they were enslaved to. Israel's deliverance did result in them being empty handed (Exodus 11: 2-3) because God made sure that they were blessed with some of the harvest of the Egyptians. Durham makes the point that

> "The Israelites "ask," and the Egyptians, in a kind of trance of affection and trust caused by Yahweh, freely give. The Egyptians thus are "picked clean" (3:22 and 12:36) by Israel as a result of yet another action by Yahweh in behalf of his people, demonstrating the power of his Presence."[117]

Yahweh delivered Israel so that they could serve him with the blessings that he had given them. He wanted the first fruit that they had received as a nation and people to be given to Him. However, because the children of Israel were so steeped in idolatry it was not long after they left Egypt (Exodus 32) that they fell back into the deep-seated things of Babylon that they had learnt.

While Moses was on the mount receiving the commands of Yahweh, the people were using the blessing they received at the hand of God to return to the very way of life God had taken them out of—idolatry. It is the normal tendency for humans to become idolatrous of that which God has blessed them with and He constantly warns against it. Deuteronomy 6:10-12 reads, "*So it shall be, when the Lord your God brings you into the land of which He swore to your fathers, to Abraham, Isaac, and Jacob, to give you large and beautiful cities which you did not build, houses full of all good things, which you did not fill, hewn-out wells which you did not dig, vineyards and olive trees which you did not plant—when you have eaten and are full—then beware, lest you forget the Lord who brought you out of the land of Egypt, from the house*

---

[117] Durham, J. I. 2002. Vol. 3: Word Biblical Commentary: Exodus. Word Biblical Commentary. Word, Incorporated: Dallas.

of bondage." When God saw that they were engaging in idol worship he commanded (Exodus 32) Moses to go down and see what was happening, then Moses interceded on behalf of the people so that God would not destroy them. However, Moses commanded the reaping of those on the Lord's side (to stand with him) and the killing of those who would continue in rebellion against God. Verse 28 notes that three thousand souls fell to the ground.

Note a comparison on the day of Pentecost in Acts 2. However, unlike the three thousand souls that were lost, here in the New Testament three thousand souls were saved. Three thousand souls were lost from differing nations that came out of Egypt while three thousand souls were saved who heard the truth of God in their own language. They accepted the spirit of the law. Some have ascribed the various languages as an initial sign for speaking in tongues as being practiced among evangelicals. Tongues are known languages and, therefore, the practice of *glossa* or tongues speaking is a pagan practice and should not be practiced by Christians. "That what was spoken with tongues was intelligible to those who understood foreign languages, as appears from Acts 2:11. Therefore, the speaking was not an incoherent, unintelligible rhapsody."[118] The cloven tongues of fire were the Spirit's power enabling persons called to witness to others of various nations and languages about the love of the Eternal. They are not signs that one has God's Holy Spirit as the Spirit of God does not contradict the truths of God and those who practice such are in violation

---

[118] Hodge, C. 2000. An Exposition of First Corinthians (electronic ed.). Ephesians Four Group: Escondito, California

of the truth of the Eternal God. Notice in Acts 2:6 that each heard someone speaking in his own language. Language is what defines humanity from all other created beings and there are numerous languages, but the one language that binds all is the language of love, "the lubricant of the spirit. The exercise of spiritual gifts without love will cause friction in the family of God and frustrate the purposes of God."[119] Therefore, the universality of the language of God (love) was spoken at Pentecost and will be proclaimed continually as a witness until He comes.

In 1 Corinthians 14, Paul addresses the issue of tongues but he was not advocating for the literal practice of *glossa* in the church. In 1 Corinthians 12 Paul mentioned that speaking in tongues and interpretation the tongues spoken are gifts for the edifying of the body of Christ and not for self-gratification. In 1 Corinthians14:2 Paul used sarcasm to address the matter. He notes that "he who speaks in a tongue does not speak to men but to God, for no one understands him.' Paul is saying only God knows what he is saying. If the gifts are given for the edifying of the body of believers, why speak to God in babbling language openly that no one can understand and it is not offered as a prayer or a benefit to the believers? It is no use and profits no one including the babbler. In verse 5 of chapter 14 Paul made a request, *"I wish you all spoke with tongues,* **not in tongues**. Paul is acknowledging "that only some have the spiritual gift and then responsibility to use it in a public ministry

---

[119] Hayford, J. W., & Curtis, G. 1997, c1994. Pathways to Pure Power: Learning the depth of love's power, a study of first Corinthians. C1994 by Jack W. Hayford. Spirit-Filled Life Bible Discovery Guides. Thomas Nelson: Nashville 272

(12:30; 14:26-28)".[120] Turn your attention to 1 Corinthians 14: 20-25. Paul asked that they be not babes in their understanding but to be mature. Why? Verse 21 answers the question, because "In the law it is written: "with men of other tongues and other lips I will speak to this people; and yet, for all that, they would not hear Me, says the Lord. Paul was quoting from Isaiah 28:11-12.**Therefore** tongues are for a sign not to those who believe but to unbelievers . . ." Tongues in Acts 2 were a sign to the unbelievers showing that there is no God like Israel's God. Paul emphasized prophecy because "prophesying is not for unbelievers but for those who believe." Prophecy convicts the believer of the truth of Yahweh so they can truly worship the God among them. God is calling peoples from all languages; those who will listen and hear and not harden their hearts (Hebrews 4:7) to the one message of the Gospel—a testimony of the love of God through Jesus Christ.

After the children of Israel were settled in their land God illustrated how they should now keep the Feast of the First Fruits/Weeks (Leviticus 23:9-14). Notable, is the fact that before the offering of the sheaves, no reaping of the harvest for personal use could be done (Leviticus 23:14). A portion of the wave-sheaf was placed on the altar and the rest eaten by the priest with the accompaniment of a male lamb sacrificed as a burnt offering. Similar to the other feasts, a special offering was made. The special cereal offering consisting of 'two loaves of bread' (Leviticus 23:17) was made with flour milled from new wheat crop

[120] Hayford, J. W., & Curtis, G. 1997, c1994. Pathways to pure power: Learning the depth of love's power, a study of first Corinthians. C1994 by Jack W. Hayford. Spirit-Filled Life Bible Discovery Guides. Thomas Nelson: Nashville

and baked with leaven. The loaves were presented as a wave offering on behalf of all the people but none of the bread was placed on the altar because it was baked with leaven. Note carefully that while the bread used at Passover and the Feast of Unleavened Bread (Exodus 12:15, 19-20; Leviticus 2:1, 4-5) were baked without leaven, at Pentecost, the loaves (which represent Israel and the saints) waved for acceptance were baked with leaven. Leaven is symbolic of sin; thus, an unleavened offering represents that which had no sin. Christ, who was without sin gives power to overcome sin, so that the salvation blessing of the wheat harvest may come to all peoples. In God's Festivals in Scripture and History the author notes that the reason for the difference in the "two loaves offered at Pentecost represented Israel's response to the blessing of salvation. Though Israel was called by God to be holy unto Him, sin still existed in the lives of the people."[121]

The acceptance of the wave-sheaf shows "the consecration of the first fruits *and* sanctifies the whole harvest, since the part stands for the whole"[122] through the process that leads to our adoption through the spirit (Romans 8:15). In Romans 11:16 Paul puts it this way, *"for if the first fruit is holy, the lump is also holy; and if the root is holy, so are the branches."* Thomas Schreiner points out that "the hallowing of the firstfruits also consecrated the rest of the batch of dough . . . if the root is consecrated, so

---

[121] Bacchiocchi, Samule (1995). God's Festivals in Scripture and History. Biblical Perspectives. Berrien Spring, Michigan 176

[122] Bacchiocchi, Samuele. 1995. God's Festivals in Scripture and History: Part 1 The Spring Festivals. Biblical Perspectives. Berrien Springs, Michigan. 172.

are the branches . . . ."[123] All saints are presently in a state of sanctification (1 Corinthians 6:11; Ephesians 5:26-27) as we await the sonship/adoption (Romans 8:23) and the redemption of our bodies. Israel's call from a lifestyle of idolatry was based on a promise God made to Abraham. Israel was holy to the Lord, the first fruits of his harvest (Jeremiah 2:3; Hosea 9:10), because it was called by God to exercise a sanctifying influence on all nations. Similarly, Christians are "a kind of first fruits of his creatures' (James 1:18; Rev. 14: 4), because as saints we are called to be a sanctifying influence in the world"[124] through the power of God's Holy Spirit. God is the one who calls people to His harvest (John 6:44) and controls the timing and reaping of the harvest. This does not negate the Christian responsibility of evangelism but firmly upholds it. Israel was called to be a light to the nations and Christians (the spiritual Israel of God) are the only reflectors of Christ's light (1 John 1:7; Matthew 5:15). It is incumbent on those who are called to tell the nations the truth which God has so graciously blessed them with, because salvation is for everyone who believes—to the Jews first and also to the Gentiles. (Romans 1:16) However, people will not know what the truth is unless it is proclaimed so that all nations and peoples of the world will hear and through the awakening of their conscience, serve the true and living God. God gave His Spirit on Pentecost, by performing "a miracle as a sign or indication that He was doing something new. Followers of Jesus were given the ability to speak in other

---

[123] Schreiner. Thomas R. 1998. Romans. Baker Academic. Baker Book House. Grand Rapids, Michigan. 599-600.

[124] Bacchiocchi, Samuele. 1995. God's Festivals in Scripture and History: Part 1 The Spring Festivals. Biblical Perspectives. Berrien Springs, Michigan. 172.

languages so that they could proclaim the Good News of the Messiah to . . . all nations."[125] Jesus, after being presented as a wave-sheaf offering to the Father, commissioned His disciples in Matthew 28: 18-20, saying *"All authority has been given to Me in heaven and on earth. Go therefore and make disciples of all the nations, baptizing them in the name of the Father and of the Son and of the Holy Spirit, teaching them to observe all things that I have commanded you; and lo, I am with you always, even to the end of the age."* Paul in Romans 10:14 also confirmed the commission when he asked the rhetorical questions, *"How then shall they call on Him in whom they have not believed? And how can they believe in Him of whom they have not heard? And how can they hear without a preacher? And how shall they preach, unless they are sent?"* The commission is to make ready souls for the eternal harvest through the gifts (1 Corinthians 12) received of the Spirit of God. Thus Pentecost is not only about the "the birth of the nation but a symbol for God's higher design in providing for the birth of a soul."[126]

Important to the meaning of Pentecost is the prophetic fulfilment of the reaping of souls as mentioned before. In 1 Corinthians 15: 20-23, Paul calls Christ's resurrection the first fruits of those who will rise from the dead. *"But now Christ is risen from the dead, and has become the first of the first fruits of those who have fallen asleep. For since by man came death, by man also came the resurrection of the dead. For as in Adam all die, even so in Christ all shall be made*

---

125 Scott, B. 1997. The Feasts of Israel (electroniced.). The Friends of Israel Gospel Ministry, Inc.: Bellmawr, New Jersey

126 McQuaid, E. 1986. The Outpouring: Jesus in the feasts of Israel. Moody Press: Chicago

alive. But each one in his own order: Christ the first fruit, afterward those who are Christ's at His coming." Note that Paul speaks twice of Christ as the first fruit not only to indicate that "He was the first to rise . . . from the grave, but also that by so doing He fulfilled the offering of the first fruits."[127] Let's recall that the first sheaf of the barley harvest (*omer*) was waved before the Lord by the priest, as a pledge of the full harvest that would follow. This wave-sheaf is none other than Christ, the "first fruit"; from the dead (1 Corinthians 15:20). Seeing that, the first sheaf was a pledge and assurance of the ingathering of the entire harvest, so the resurrection of Christ is an assurance that all who put their faith in Him will be raised from the dead. This faith is active (James 2: 20) and must see the believer participating in the work of God as Christ did.

In Matthew 13:1-23 we see the parable of the different types of soil being mentioned. Christ used agriculture to show persons' response to the truth. Therefore, it is more than just an agricultural custom. Notice His answer to the disciples when asked why He spoke in parables (v10-11)—"*Because it has been given to you to know the mysteries of the kingdom of heaven, but to them it has not been given.'* 'God has granted the disciples, "to know the mysteries of the kingdom of heaven"; to the crowds ("to them") he has not granted this."[128] Christ used the parable of the field to show the selectivity of the called and what will

---

[127] Bacchiocchi, Samuele. 1995. God's Festivals in Scripture and History: Part 1 The Spring Festivals. Biblical Perspectives. Berrien Springs, Michigan. 173

[128] Hagner, D. A. 2002. Vol. 33A: Word Biblical Commentary: Matthew 1-13. Word Biblical Commentary. Word, Incorporated: Dallas

happen to the harvest. He is coming back for his property and the souls that are ready at the harvest (John 4:35). Not all will understand the mysteries of God; only those to whom God has placed the truth in their heart through the call and the gift of God's Holy Spirit and bears the fruit of righteousness. (2 Thessalonians 2:13-14; 1 Peter 1:22)

Pentecost was a joyous occasion represented by a holy convocation which called for the abstention from work (Leviticus 23:21). Liberation from the hardship of life and social inequalities of Egypt was both physical and spiritual and illustrate how Israel was, in turn, to treat their slaves in the land which they would possess. This confirms the command to '*love thy neighbour as thyself*' (Leviticus 19:18; Romans 13:9; Galatians 5:14) and can only happen when the love of God has entered the hearts of mankind to live in obedience to His will. It is living out the meaning of Pentecost in our everyday lives as our inner man is being renewed daily by God's Holy Spirit (2 Corinthians 4:16).

The story of Ruth, which was read at Pentecost, is a profound picture of what God is doing through the harvest. J. V. McGee states "the Book of Ruth is a laboratory demonstration that "the greatest of these is love" (1 Cor. 13:13)."[129] The story is about two women representing two nations—Jews and Gentiles; and the universal language of love which brought them together as one despite their differences. Ruth was a Moabite. "Moab was the son of Lot by incestuous union with his eldest daughter (Gn. 19:37)."[130]

---

[129] McGee, J. V. 2001, c1988. Ruth and Esther: Women of faith (electronic ed.). Thomas Nelson Publishers: Nashville

[130] Wood, D. R. W., Wood, D. R. W., & Marshall, I. H. 1996, c1982, c1962. New Bible Dictionary. Includes index.

Elimelech and his wife Naomi were natives of Bethlehem Judah but journeyed to the land of Moab with both their sons at a time when there was spiritual and moral decay in Israel. Both sons married women from Moab but both died leaving Naomi to return to the land and the God of her salvation. However, she did not return alone, as one of her daughters-in-law followed her. They return to Bethlehem at the beginning of the barley harvest. (Ruth 1:22) Remember that the Passover depicts one turning away from sin and a return to the God who invites both Jews and Gentiles to the harvesting of souls. Like Abraham, who left his own land, people and god, Ruth went to join a people and worship a God she did not know (Ruth 2:11-12). Hayford etal note

> "Ruth, a Moabitess, willingly leaves her homeland and places her future in the hands of the God of Israel. Instead of recoiling from the stark reality of Noami's financial, emotional, social, and spiritual condition, Ruth clings to Naomi in steadfast personal commitment. In so doing, Ruth's personal commitment becomes a picture of Christ."[131]

Keep in mind that the Eternal God is the reaper of the harvest and Boaz is a type of Christ who saw in Ruth a love that is a type to that of God. He is the kinsman Redeemer at work. "Redemption is possible only through the Kinsman-Redeemer. God could not redeem apart

---

(electronic ed. of 3rd ed.) . InterVarsity Press: Downers Grove. 775

[131] Hayford, J. W., & Hagen, K. A. 1997, c1996. Redemption and Restoration: Reversing life's greatest losses, a study of Ruth and Esther. C1996 by Jack W. Hayford. Spirit-Filled Life Bible Discovery Guides. Thomas Nelson: Nashville

from a Mediator, and since only God could redeem, it was necessary for Him to become that Person."[132] In 1 John 4, the author points out that no one has seen God at anytime and for His love to abide in us through His Spirit, we ought to love as God loves because God is love. Notice the similarity with feet. Naomi told Ruth to uncover the feet of Boaz when he was sleeping. J. V. McGee notes,

> "Ruth reinforces the symbolism of respectful humility demonstrated by her position at Boaz's feet by identifying herself as "your maidservant" (v. 9). Borrowing a phrase from Boaz's prayer uttered that first day in the field (2:12), Ruth pleads, "Take your maidservant under your wing."[133] 'Naomi looks beyond the letter of the Law and asks Boaz to perform God's heart intent in the Law: "that human loss always be recoverable and that we work with Him in extending such possibilities to those in need."[134]

This love is what has perfected the law as the *omer* went up to God as a sweet smelling savour. It is what will enable us to enter the Kingdom of the Eternal God.

---

[132] McGee, J. V. 2001, c1988. Ruth and Esther: Women of faith (electronic ed.). Thomas Nelson Publishers: Nashville 41

[133] Hayford, J. W., & Hagen, K. A. 1997, c1996. Redemption and restoration : Reversing life's greatest losses, a study of Ruth and Esther. C1996 by Jack W. Hayford. Spirit-Filled Life Bible Discovery Guides. Thomas Nelson: Nashville

[134] Hayford, J. W., & Hagen, K. A. 1997, c1996. Redemption and restoration : Reversing life's greatest losses, a study of Ruth and Esther. C1996 by Jack W. Hayford. Spirit-Filled Life Bible Discovery Guides. Thomas Nelson: Nashville

Pentecost saw Israel's birth as a nation, a spiritual people consecrated unto God and represents the church—the spiritual Israel in the New Testament. It was the call and seal of the power of God's Holy Spirit that qualified Israel as a nation and qualifies the Church of God today as God does not give His Spirit to those who do not obey Him (Acts 5:32). The nation of Israel was not all Israelites but an organised body that God gave a commission. "Pentecost reminds us that the Christian church was founded by Christ, not to perpetuate itself as a self-serving organization but to extend the divine provision of salvation to men and women everywhere."[135] (Some of the nations including Egyptians became converts due to the miraculous signs of deliverance by Yahweh). In like manner, so it is with the mission of the Christian church in this era which is "an organized body of believers with a message and a mission"[136] (Matthew 28:19-20). The prophetic vision and fulfilment "of the ingathering of God's people from all the nations to the uplifted temple in Zion and the going forth of the command to teach all nations is depicted by this feast of the first fruits. (Is. 2: 2-3; Mic. 4: 1-2; John 2:19; 12:32)."[137] After Christ's resurrection, He told his disciples to tarry in Jerusalem until God's Holy Spirit energized them so that they would become His witnesses even to the end of the earth (Acts 1: 8). Like the Israelites, the people at Pentecost all witnessed the power of God when cloven tongues of fire fell on the apostles and those gathered. Acts 2:5 which states "*devout men from every nation under heaven*" not only

---

[135] Bacchiocchi, Samuele. 1995. God's Festivals in Scripture and History: Part 1 The Spring Festivals. Biblical Perspectives. Berrien Springs, Michigan. 194

[136] ibid 192

[137] ibid 192

underscores the Christian mission but also expresses the desire of Yahweh that each language group should hear, in its native language, the message most meaningful to the human heart—love.

The significance of the bestowal of gifts is also a mark of Pentecost, so that each may participate in the life and mission of the church. Recall the earlier discussion on the body—all performing different functions. This is highlighted by the gifts spoken of in 1 Corinthians 12 which are for the building up of the body of Christ (Ephesians 4:12). Before His death, Christ reassured His disciples that he would bestow upon them the gift of God's Holy Spirit—the gift that would bring within their reach the boundless resources of His grace—His love. John 14: 16-17 states "*I will pray the Father, and He will give you another Helper, that He may abide with you forever—the Spirit of truth, whom the world cannot receive, because it neither sees Him nor knows Him; but you know Him, for He dwells with you, and will be in you.*" Christ was pointing to the day when the Holy Spirit of God would come to do a mighty work—showing the saints what really makes them unique. The prophecy of Joel 2:28-32 showing that both men and women would be involved in the process of the reaping souls is also a fulfilment of Pentecost. It challenges the saints to constantly examine their conduct and to recognize that they are "called to the full-time task of proclaiming 'the wonderful deeds of Him who called us out of darkness into His marvellous light (1 Pet. 2:9)."[138] All the redeemed can receive the spiritual

---

[138]   Bacchiocchi, Samuele. 1995. God's Festivals in Scripture and History: Part 1 The Spring Festivals. Biblical Perspectives. Berrien Springs, Michigan. 194

gifts that equip the saints for the work of ministry. This is made possible through the Comforter, given at Pentecost and has been granted to all who have yielded themselves to the transforming power of redeeming love (Acts 5:32). "The mission of God's Holy Spirit will continue until the Gospel has been preached to all nations (Matt 24:24)."[139] It challenges us to pray daily for the endowment of spiritual power to become fit labourers (Matthew 9: 37-38) together with God in the final harvest at the millennium.

Pentecost also underscores the ministry of Jesus Christ as the mediator (1Timothy 2:5). "Christ is the mediator of a better covenant (Hebrews 8:6; 9:15; 12:24). In (Acts 5: 31; 1 John 2:1-2; 1:9), we see where Christ intercedes for forgiveness on behalf of believers, (John 16:23-24; Revelation 8:3), makes prayers acceptable to God the Father, and provides the invisible, assistance of His angels (Daniel 6:28; Acts 5:19; Hebrews 1:14) on our behalf."[140] According to His promise, He had sent the Holy Spirit from heaven to His followers as a token that He had, as Priest and King, received all authority in heaven and on earth, and was the Anointed One over His people.

Christ himself is the first of first fruits symbolized by Pentecost and also reminds us of the final resurrection harvest to come. Paul in Romans 8:22-23 states 'For *we know that the whole creation groans and labours with birth*

---

[139] Bacchiocchi, Samuele. 1995. God's Festivals in Scripture and History: Part 1 The Spring Festivals. Biblical Perspectives. Berrien Springs, Michigan. 195

[140] Bacchiocchi, Samuele. 1995. God's Festivals in Scripture and History: Part 1 The Spring Festivals. Biblical Perspectives. Berrien Springs, Michigan. 195

pangs together until now. Not only, that, but we also who have the firstfruits of the Spirit, even we ourselves groan within ourselves, eagerly waiting for adoption, the redemption of our body. As we receive the fruit of the God's Spirit, we manifest such in our lives namely: *love, joy, peace, longsuffering, kindness, goodness, faithfulness, gentleness, self-control* (Galatians 5: 22-23). James 1:18 speaks about those who are being redeemed from mankind as first fruits for God and the Lamb.

Trumpets

Jesus Christ the Trumpet Call to Righteousness

Now, there are some other Feasts/Holy Days that tell who the Almighty God is through the person of Jesus Christ. These are termed "the Fall Holy Days" and considered a culmination of the spring festivals discussed earlier. Of importance is the fact that Jesus Christ, coming in human flesh, was a Trumpet call, Atonement and Tabernacle, all depicting the conclusion of God's redemptive plan. The end of the spring harvest season was ushered in by the Feast of Trumpets also known as Rosh Hashanah which fell on the first day of the seventh month known as Tishri. The blowing of trumpets is characteristic of this day as trumpets were used for signals based upon their varying sound patterns: to assemble the people together (Numbers10:2, 3-4, 7; Judges 3:27); for times of travel (Numbers10: 2, 5, 6) and even for war (Numbers10:9; 31:6-7).

In the New Testament, the themes, though not explicitly stated, continue to fulfil those of the Old Testament but more firmly represent Jesus Christ as the trumpet sound to a righteous life in obedience to the will of God the Father. Jesus' life was the preaching (and living) of the Gospel and the proclamation of God's government soon-to-be established here on earth. Because the blowing of trumpets was associated with the arousal from sleep and the announcement of imminent danger (Amos 3:6; Ezekiel 33: 1-16), it is now the primary responsibility of the saints to sound the trumpet (Isaiah 58:1) to awaken those souls who are in spiritual slumber and are exposed to impending danger. Christ's life and death serve to awaken the souls of the world to the Spirit of life and peace. Keep in mind that it is the soul that died and thus needs to be rescued from its grim existence. "Rosh Hashanah (meaning *Head* or *Beginning of the Year*) is also known by three other names: The Day of Judgement, the Day of the Sounding of the Shofar (ram's horn), and the Day of Remembrance."[141]

The Feast of Trumpets represents a day of judgement and war when God will ultimately put in his appearance as ruler over the earth, thus, the need to warn. According to McQuaid

> "It was believed by the Jews of the period that Rosh Hashanah was the day when God judged mankind. They believed "the judgment commenced immediately after the Jewish Sanhedrin had settled that the new moon of Tishri had actually risen." Any aspect of rejoicing was in anticipation of Jehovah's mercy's being extended to penitents."[142]

The book of Revelation closes the Bible well with these themes as it gives evidence to and announces the return of Jesus Christ to earth as King of Kings with the summoning of The seventh trumpet. The blowing of trumpets did not always reflect judgement and vindication but also signified triumph and happiness (Joshua 6:20; 1 Chronicles 13:8; 15: 24, 28; 2 Chronicles 5:13).

---

[141] Scott, Bruce. 1997. The Feasts of Israel (electroniced.). The Friends of Israel Gospel Ministry, Inc.: Bellmawr, New Jersey
[142] McQuaid, E. 1986. The Outpouring: Jesus in the feasts of Israel. Moody Press: Chicago

Trumpets were made from various materials such as silver (Numbers 10: 2) and rams' horns (Joshua 6:8) but it is the shofar or ram's horn that was blown on the Feast of Trumpets. The loud blowing of the shofar on this day is to be understood as signifying 'the beginning of trial before the heavenly court, a trial that lasted ten days until the Day of Atonement.'[143] Bruce Scott pointed out,

> "The judgment handed down on that day, with its subsequent recording in the Book of Life, decides a person's fate in this life for the coming year. That is not to say that people's actions do not impact the final judgment of their souls after they die, but on Rosh Hashanah their behavior is judged only for the here and now and not for the hereafter."[144]

On the tenth day came the Day of Atonement when God would dispose of sin permanently and it was also a call to reassure the Israelites that God would remember and vindicate them on this particular day of judgement. The ten days of repentance calls for meditation to discipline the mind from distractions. It is only when the mind can remain focused for significant periods of time that it can be brought into alignment with its true purpose at the Atonement; the state in which it was at the beginning, before sin.

---

[143]   Bacchiocchi, Samuele. 1996. God's Festivals in Scripture and History: Part 2 The Fall Festivals. Biblical Perspectives. Berrien Springs, Michigan. 58

[144]   Scott, Bruce. 1997. The Feasts of Israel (electroniced.). The Friends of Israel Gospel Ministry, Inc.: Bellmawr, New Jersey

The blowing of Trumpets was not new to the children of Israel as each month at the new moon trumpets were blown (Numbers 10:10) and this was understood as a miniature day of judgement, which warned the people to prepare for the final judgement of their souls. "During the new moons of the first six months, the trumpets were blown to warn the people about the forthcoming judgement but on the new moon of the seventh month, the trumpets were blown to announce the inauguration of the heavenly bodies."[145] Note in revelation the blowing of seven trumpets and it was at the seventh trumpet that Jesus will return. The Feast of Trumpets reveals that "God has a heart to warn His people because He is not in the business to punish but to save."[146] He uses attention-catching methods (Revelation 9:20; 16:9) to warn and lead His people to repentance before executing judgement (Revelation 14:7) and it was designed to channel the reconnection of soul and spirit for alignment and balancing.

Interestingly, this feast, unlike the others, was a time of uncertainty due to the fact that no one knew when the new moon would appear, (Note a comparison with Matthew 24:36; 1 Thessalonians 5: 1-11) as "Rosh Hashanah is the only Jewish holiday celebrated on a new moon (the first of the month), in the month Tishri."[147] Though the new

---

[145] Bacchiocchi, Samuele. 1996. God's Festivals in Scripture and History: Part 2The Fall Festivals. Biblical Perspectives. Berrien Springs, Michigan. 42-43

[146] Bacchiocchi, Samuele. 1996. God's Festivals in Scripture and History: Part 2The Fall Festivals. Biblical Perspectives. Berrien Springs, Michigan. 81

[147] The Feasts of Israel (electroniced.). The Friends of Israel Gospel Ministry, Inc.: Bellmawr, New Jersey

month was scheduled to start, if the new moon did not accompany the new month there would be no trumpet blowing. This was also the reason the Feast of Trumpets was kept for two days instead of a predated format that is now being followed. Today; the uncertainty of the time brings into sharp focus of the message of the Gospel, which informs us to always be prepared for the return of the Lord Jesus Christ. Christ warned in Matthew 24:42, 44 of His return and regarding the impending danger 'watch therefore, for you do not know what hour your Lord is coming.' No one knows the day or the hour and, as a result, the command to watch. The God of heaven is trumpeting the call to repentance for all peoples. In Revelation 12:1 we see 'a woman clothed with the sun, with the moon under her feet.' Note the mention of feet again associated with a woman who at times is identified as the bride of Christ which represents the church (Revelation 19:7-8; 21:9-10). This woman bears a Child, which is none other than Jesus Christ. It is the 'church' that continues to preach the Gospel of the coming Kingdom of God signified by the moon as the time marker/sign of those who walk in obedience to the Eternal. This woman is the church that is trumpeting the call to repentance and life and will be persecuted for it.

Another interesting point to the command to watch which is very significant, is that at the time of the Jews, there were two witnesses who would watch to see when the moon appears and warn the people, who were already assembled, by sounding the trumpet. The people had no time to wait and needed to be kept on the alert hence, the significance of the parable of the wise and foolish virgins in Matthew 25:1-13. At the sounding of the trumpet the bridegroom will come and after a time the door would be shut. Hagner in commenting notes,

> "The kingdom of heaven is likened not to the virgins but to the story of what happens to them: when the sudden arrival occurs, some are ready and some are not . . . . The focus of the parable is the simple matter of preparedness versus unpreparedness and the tragic character of the latter."[148]

At the midnight cry the bridegroom comes so He can marry His bride. This bridegroom is none other than Christ Jesus and is coming for His prepared bride (the church) who is adorned for her husband (Revelation 21:2). Only those prepared will be able to enter the marriage banquet. Note in verse 8 that "the foolish virgins, by being unprepared for the coming of the bridegroom with its unanticipated delay, are shut out from enjoying the wedding banquet, and no appeal can change that reality."[149]

In Revelation 16:15, John, on the isle of Patmos, made reference to the dual nature of the command: salvation and judgement. It reads *"Behold, I am coming as a thief. Blessed is he who watches, and keeps his garments, lest he walk naked and they see his shame"*. Not that Christ is a thief but as Aune commented "the motif of watchfulness in expectation of the sudden eschatological consummation occurs elsewhere.

---

[148]   Hagner, D. A. 2002. Vol. 33B: Word Biblical Commentary: Matthew 14-28. Word Biblical Commentary. Word, Incorporated: Dallas

[149]   Hagner, D. A. 2002. Vol. 33B: Word Biblical Commentary: Matthew 14-28. Word Biblical Commentary. Word, Incorporated: Dallas

In Revelation only, in 3:2-3, where it is combined with the threat that Jesus will come as a thief in the event that Christians fail to be watchful."[150] The command carries a blessing if garments are kept on and shame if found without them. It was a custom for the priest to watch and not fall asleep. This relates to Adam in the Garden of Eden. When called of God to see whether he had acted righteously or not; he reported, "I was afraid and hid myself because I was naked and neglected the command thou gavest and I was ashamed." Those who will be found naked are those who have neglected the sign and to do the command of Yahweh like Adam did, bringing condemnation on themselves. The first man was to be a light of righteousness to all people but failed. Christ, the second Adam, came to be that trumpet call to a righteous life.

The call to live righteously never stopped with the fall of Adam but continued through Abraham and the subsequent nation of Israel whom God chose to be the guiding light to world. The blowing of the first six trumpets in the book of Revelation warns people everywhere to prepare for the final judgement and war which is represented by the sounding of the seventh and final trumpet. God will declare war on those who fail to keep his commandments. Some have largely focused on the seventh trumpet not realizing the significance of the first six. The first six trumpets predict ecological disasters that will affect every aspect of human life. Just as the economy of Egypt was affected by the environmental catastrophes that struck the land so will it

---

[150] Aune, D. E. 2002. Vol. 52B: Word Biblical Commentary: Revelation 6-16. Word Biblical Commentary. Word, Incorporated: Dallas

happen in the days to come. God blew the trumpets for the saints' preparation in leaving Babylon and He constantly makes that call. When the children of Israel were in Egypt, the trumpet blowing was significant in the plagues that were affecting the Egyptians and for the children of Israel to prepare to leave captivity for freedom. The themes are the same and if one should take a look at the plagues of the six trumpets in revelation and those at the time of the Exodus experience one will note a striking similarity. The signs were a preparation for their deliverance and should be a fearful experience but were also a joyous one because God had heard their cry and would not leave them to the mercy of the enemy. In Revelation 8 the signs which appeared at the blown trumpets correspond to those of the Exodus, signalling that God would make a final end of the Egyptians and this world, ushering in the world to come (Revelation 11:15). Christ counselled, 'now when these things begin to happen, look up and lift up your heads, because your redemption draws near (Luke 21:28).

Revelation 8-11 tells us about the trumpets and their destruction. They tell of God's warning of impending judgement. Chapter 8:7 we see the first trumpet with destruction of vegetation similar to the seventh plague in Egypt (Exodus 9: 22-23). Already, the world is experiencing numerous and frequent hurricanes that will increase as the end draws nearer, destroying crops and lands that are suitable for cultivating food items causing famine and hunger. The second trumpet (8: 8-9) saw the attack on the seas with the waters turning to blood—similar to the first plague on Egypt (Exodus 7:14). The fact that the world is experiencing a shortage of pure drinking water due to pollution is enough to tell that the situation will only get worse. Revelation 9: 1-12 saw the fifth trumpet announcing the locusts on the land comparative to the eighth in Exodus 10. These signs show the power of Yahweh; a revelation of Himself to unbelievers. In Exodus 7:9; 9:16; 10:1, God used these signs to show who He was to Pharaoh who paraded himself as a god. He will do the same in times to come as He demonstrates that He is the only God who deserves worship.

Every time a believer answers the call of God to live righteously and do the command spoken of in Matthew 28:19, he is symbolically sounding the trumpet of the Eternal God. It symbolizes the saints' resurrection from dead works, and the future resurrection of the dead who die in Christ. God raised (Acts 13:30; Galatians 1:1; Colossians 2:12; 1 Peter 1:21) Christ from the dead on the third day. It is the change of all who are alive in Christ at His second coming (1 Corinthians 15: 21-23). It is a signal of promise that through our blowing of trumpets (prayer and righteous life), the saints remind the Eternal God that He promised not to leave them to the will of the enemy. The return of Christ and the gathering of God's elect (Matthew 24:31) elevate the minds of the saints to their true hope and destiny. It is a warning to saints to get their houses (souls) in order for judgement on the Day of Atonement when the called will either be reunited with God or damned to hell. Jesus Christ is symbolically that Trumpet blast signalling the incarnation represented by the atonement; a most remarkable event in history. The trumpet reminds the saints, as it did Israel, to have faith in the future coming of the Messiah and the gathering of His people. Christ has awakened the souls of the saints to the truth that was lost at the beginning. Will you heed the call?

Remember, mankind was estranged from his true home and his desire is for that home from which he was separated. Thus, the blowing of trumpets also signifies an act of crying out to God in time of great need and homesickness. The soul longs to be with God the Father and Jesus Christ from whom it was separated. The soul can only be reconciled through the atonement and Christ is the atoning sacrifice.

The Atonement

Jesus Christ the reconciler of mankind

The culmination of the ten days of repentance (Days of Awe) ushered in by the Feast of Trumpets ended on the Day of Atonement, the day when judgment was pronounced. Commonly known as Yom Kippur or the Fast (Acts 27:9). It is said to be the holiest day of the year and was celebrated with prohibitions regarding labour, eating, drinking, anointing, the wearing of sandals and marital intercourse. These ritual prohibitions concluded the atoning process (Leviticus 16:16, 30, 34) and were designed to show that sin was an unwelcome intrusion in the life of the people of God. The rituals of the "Feast Days" taught that before sin could be permanently cleansed and disposed of, they had to be repented of, forsaken and a judgement made by the heavenly court. Remember the first Adam died and through the power of God's Holy Spirit, given at Pentecost, all are called to life from dead works (Ephesians 2:1; Colossians 1:21) to serve the true and living God.

On this day the priest entered the Holy of Holies of the tabernacle to make atonement for the sins committed by himself, his family and the nation of Israel. The Priest acted on behalf of God and the nation of Israel. Thus the cleansing of the sanctuary was carried out and represented the government of God. Bacchiocchi mentions that "sin defiles the sanctuary because it is a transgression of the principles of God's government. When God's principles are transgressed,

the sanctuary is . . . defiled by the objective reality of sin."[151]
The temple or sanctuary is the abiding place for God; which
the New Testament associates with our bodies. It is because
sin separates us why God is not able to dwell with us. The
atonement is what gives us new access. Second Corinthians
5:17 says, *"Therefore, if anyone is in Christ, he is a new
creation; old things have passed away; behold, all things have
become new,"* giving man, the pinnacle of God's creation,
a new status in the atonement. Christ's death is a covering
for the sin of humanity with the aim of reconciling man
to God through repentance and forgiveness. In looking at
the Feast of Trumpets, we realize that the blowing of the
trumpets was a call to repentance and emphasized man's
return to God. God is warning people everywhere to return
to Him. All of God's people, then and now, are called to
assemble before Him as this day was proclaimed as a holy
convocation (Leviticus 23:27-28; Numbers 29:7) to abstain
from the known prohibitions and cleanse their souls before
Him. The abstention from physical food was to teach
His people that man does not live by bread alone but by
every word of God (Deuteronomy 8:3; Matthew 4:4). It
acknowledges the insufficiency of bread alone without the
will to please the Father as demonstrated by Christ who
came to do the will of the Father (John 4:34). It was the
desire for food that saw Adam and Eve not taking God at
His word rejecting His will.

Though this day was celebrated with a fast, it was a
day with just as much rejoicing as on this day souls were

[151] Bacchiocchi, Samuele. 1996. God's Festivals in Scripture
and History: Part 2 The Fall Festivals. Biblical Perspectives.
Berrien Springs, Michigan. 130.

released from bondage and brought in union with God. The word "atone" means to reconcile, appease, pacify or purge. The sin of humanity at the beginning brought a separation as mankind became enemies of God (Romans 5:10-11). However, a way was made possible (Leviticus 17:11) so mankind can now be reconciled to God. The rituals performed in the temple must not be seen as mere symbolic rites as the sacrifices offered were representative of the souls of the people on the altar of sacrifice by the lives of the animals. (The altar is the accepting place for sacrifices and represents the mind of God). Each household was required to take their own animal sacrifice. When Adam and Eve disobeyed God, the temple (body) was invaded by evil or sin which we are asked to unleavened during the days of Unleavened Bread so that the Spirit of God can abide with us through the acceptance of the wave-sheaf at Pentecost. The temple, at the time, was polluted with the sins of the people and God chose to cleanse it on the Day of Atonement so that He could dwell among His people. Also, by feeling that their sins were removed, they could rejoice before God and would leave feeling strong enough to begin healing their clouded minds, enabling them to protect themselves from the enemy of their souls.

On this day no one was permitted to be in the tabernacle except the high priest (Leviticus 16:17) and he could not enter the Holies of Holy as he wished; not without blood, the medium through which they could approach God. There was a line of demarcation between Yahweh and His people that was noticeable by the cloud which appeared. This cloud acted as a covering. The Priest was to make atonement for himself and the people after which he was to use two goats—one as a sin offering which he obtained by casting lots. Because both animals were goats, casting lots would tell which role each would play. After the selection of goats, the high priest would kill one of them and sprinkle its blood on and before the mercy seat, making atonement for the holy place and the children of Israel. Christ who entered the Holy of Holies once, for all, using His own blood as atonement for Himself and the whole world has replaced that high-priestly role. Take into account: a priest could not enter the Holy of Holies to offer sacrifice if he were not considered worthy; he would be killed (Hebrews 9:6-10). However, when Christ came as high priest, after the Order of Melchizedek (Hebrews 5:6; 7:17; Psalm 110:4) he was able to enter once, for all, into the Holy place with his own blood thereby obtaining/securing eternal salvation (Hebrews 9:12). Christ did not attribute the priesthood to Himself but was directly called to the office by God the Father (John 4:34; 5:30). The focus of interest is not Melchizedek who greeted and blessed Abraham with bread and wine which later became the new symbols of the Passover; but to whom the priesthood like his was promised. (Genesis 14:18-20) "The promise was fulfilled in Christ who *is* actually what Melchizedek *was* symbolically, an eternal priest who exercises his priestly prerogatives in a nonlegal, universal ministration."[152] Therefore, any reference to Melchizedek only serves to amplify the uniqueness of Christ whose priesthood was not established upon the external circumstances of birth and descent but on something better. Melchizedek was introduced for the sake of the Son of God and is both redemptive and prophetic.

---

[152] Lane, W. L. 2002. Vol. 47A: Word Biblical Commentary: Hebrews 1-8. Word Biblical Commentary. Word, Incorporated: Dallas

Christ atoning death pointed to the deficiency of the old order (the ceremonial laws of the Old Testament) and to the superiority and sufficiency of the new (Hebrews 9:14) the conscience of the believer. Though Melchizedek bears the eternal character of the Son, it is the Son who remains of primary focus as He is the heavenly High Priest of those who are awaiting salvation.

One must not forget that one of the goats was given the name (title) Azazel (scapegoat), on which all the sins of the nation were transferred as a form of punishment and was non-sacrificial. Its function was to dispose of the sins of God's people in a desert region where there is no life so that God might continue to dwell with His people. This transference helps us to understand that though humanity played a part in sin by choice, the symbols of the atonement confirm that mankind's choice was not entirely his own. Mankind was influenced by the forces of evil; the serpent who beguiled Eve (Genesis 3:4; 2 Corinthians 11: 3, 14) to question God's command. This evil force is none other than Satan, the Devil, whose task is to rob and destroy; not the physical commodities but the essence of life—our souls. The Day of Atonement foretells how this enemy of God and mankind will be destroyed and ultimately the world will be at-one-ment with God (Revelation 12:9).

The Day of Atonement is a means of making things right with our souls and our Creator so as to bring back the order and balance into the world that existed at the beginning. In Matthew 16:26 the question is asked, 'For what profit is it to a man if he gains the whole world, and loses his own soul? Or what will a man give in exchange for his soul?' Satan knows humanity's destiny is to be at-one with His Creator and Lord and will do whatever it takes to lead the saints off the straight and narrow so that their souls will not be in divine oneness with the Eternal God of the universe. Peter sounds a warning in 1 Peter 5:8, saying *"be sober, be vigilant; because your adversary the devil walks about like a roaring lion, seeking whom he may devour.* Resist him, is our command, and he will flee (James 4:7).

Recall that after becoming a soul man was given a commission to be carried out for the glory of God. Due to the fact that evil and good cannot dwell together in the same time and place, God, through the abiding presence of His Holy Spirit, is ridding the evil from the soul which will bring about humanity's complete Atonement. As Christ is one with the Father (John 10:30) so He prayed the saints will be in like manner (John 17:11). It was (is) God's desire that mankind do good and not evil but humanity chose to serve its own purpose, resulting in separation from the Eternal. Now, man is commanded to repent and not be enslaved to the enemy of evil, which will be destroyed (1 Corinthians 15:26). It is Christ's atonement that fulfils our adoption/ sonship, which will enable us to be born in the Kingdom of God by the Spirit. The adoption gives mankind legal status equal to that of Christ. God purchased humanity from the enemy, which held him captive in sin. As the Father appointed Christ heir of all things; (Hebrews 1: 2) so too will the saints be heirs of the promises of God. It is no act of our own but simply by the righteousness of God through the atoning sacrifice of His Son Jesus Christ.

When God rebuked the people spoken of in Isaiah 58 regarding their Fast, notice the reasons given had nothing to do with the cessation of the Feast Days. He did so because the spirit of love which he demands was not present. Read for yourself. It starts out by saying, *sound your voice like a trumpet and tell the people their sins.* How can the saints come before the Eternal Yahweh to be reconciled to Him without reconciling with their fellow brethren? Notice again what Yahweh says in Isaiah 58:3-4 *in the day of your fast you find pleasure.* What was their pleasure? Their pleasure was *to exploit their labourers . . . for strife and debate and to strike with the* fist of wickedness. That was not Yahweh's intention and He made that clear in verses 6-9. It reads *'Is this not the fast that I have chosen: to loose the bonds of wickedness, to undo the heavy burdens, to let the oppressed go free and that you break every yoke . . . to share your bread with the hungry . . . house the poor who are cast out.* This is what Christ did as He tabernacled here on earth. He asks nothing less. First John 3:10-15 states that no one can say they love God without loving their brother also. There was no love among the people but oppression and burdens of rituals without a true heart. Like the Pharisees in Jesus' day, they were ritualistic and legalistic; the people fasted to oppress each other. In Psalm 51:17, the sacrifices that God require are the true intent of the heart. God does not delight in sacrifices without obedience because it profits nothing. (1 Samuel 15:22)

Tabernacles

Jesus Christ the True Tabernacle

For mankind to have survived his existence, he needed somewhere to dwell/tabernacle for his temporary time here on earth. This brings us to the Feast of Tabernacles or the Feast of Ingathering (Feast of Booths) which solidifies the incarnation of God (Jesus Christ) in human flesh. The incarnation brings the concept of redemption in the atonement closer to our attention. It is not the Christmas story, but the promise of God to "once again tabernacle with His people when He returns to reign over all the world from Jerusalem (Micah 4:1-7)."[153] If the incarnation of Jesus Christ which was made possible through the Spirit of God, has no relevance except for him being wrapped in swaddling clothes then mankind has no cover for sins and his future is hopeless. Paul, in speaking of the hope we have in the resurrection of Christ, states, in 1 Corinthians 15:19; 'If in this life only we have hope in Christ, we are of all men the most pitiable.' There would be no redemption or 'passing over' (forgiveness) of sins. The forgiveness of sins was made possible through the incarnation—God being at one with human flesh.

The Feast of Tabernacles solidifies God's promise to redeem mankind and protect His people by endowing them with His Holy Spirit as they dwell in booths during their temporary sojourn in the wilderness. The body, given to mankind at the beginning of creation, was never meant

---

[153] http://www.scribd.com/doc/8616689/A-Study-on-His-Return-on-a-Jewish-Festival

to be permanent but was assigned a resting place for God sharing himself with humanity. "The Feast of Tabernacles was divinely established as a seven-day commemoration followed by a one-day "convocation" (Sabbath). In its entirety, it was actually an eight-day observance. The feast embodied three basic elements that involved Israel's past, present, and future."[154] It is spoken of as seven days in Deuteronomy 16:13, 15; Ezekiel 45:25. However, an eighth day is deemed realistic as seen in Leviticus 23:34-36; Numbers. 29: 12-39). This eighth day is a portrayal of what will happen after the millennial reign of Christ when salvation will be made open and available to all mankind. The Feast of Tabernacles was a reminder to Israel, according to Leviticus 23:42-43, that God made them to dwell in booths when He brought them out of the land of Egypt. The booths were to be temporary and symbolized the human need to depend upon God for physical, as well as spiritual, sustenance. The Feast of Booths also symbolized God's desire to dwell with mankind—God wanted a temple; a place to house the Spirit that He has given to mankind; and hence the need for temporary dwelling.

The Feast of Booths is designed to celebrate God's closeness to us—and ours to Him—as we seek to return to Him in repentance and in hope of our glorious destiny with the one in whom we live, move and have our being (Acts 17:28). The tabernacle was built as a house or place of worship for the children of Israel and was the temple where God dwelled to show the people that he will never leave or forsake them. David Levy observed that "the Tabernacle

---

[154] McQuaid, E. 1986. The Outpouring: Jesus in the feasts of Israel. Moody Press: Chicago

served as a place for God to dwell among His people and a place where His people could commune with Him (Ex. 25:8; 40:34-37)."[155] In Leviticus 23:33-43, instructions on how to keep the Feast of Tabernacles were given; along with directions on how to build these booths. Though they were provisional dwelling for the period prescribed they must not be seen as just temporary shelters in which the Israelites dwelt but also symbolized the Shekinah glory of God dwelling as a covering over his people. When the children of Israel left Egypt God was with them as a protector in the pillar of cloud (Exodus 13: 21-22). This pillar of cloud was the tabernacle of God that overshadowed the people of Israel as they journeyed through the wilderness. It was a pillar of cloud by day and a pillar of fire by night that rested over the people as they tabernacled. "They were guided in this choice by Yahweh's own Presence, symbolized by the theophanic fire, seen as a column of cloud in daylight and as a column of fire at night."[156] This cloud provided the shade by day and a guiding light at night for His people on their journey to the Promised Land. The shade is symbolic of God's Spirit that guides. His Spirit guides the saints presently called to enter the promised rest of the Eternal Kingdom.

After their settlement in the land of promise the Ark of the Covenant was where God originally tabernacled with His people. This was carried by those assigned to do so,

---

[155] Levy, D. M. 1993. The tabernacle : Shadows of the Messiah: Its sacrifices, services, and priesthood. Friends of Israel Gospel Ministry: Bellmawr, NJ

[156] Durham, J. I. 2002. Vol. 3: Word Biblical Commentary: Exodus. Word Biblical Commentary. Word, Incorporated: Dallas

until Solomon (1 Kings 6: 37-38); not David because he was stained with the blood of his enemies (1 Chronicles 22: 8), built the temple of God as a resting place. God was made to dwell in the Holy of Holies and was seen on the Day of Atonement when He appeared to the priest in a pillar of cloud to show His presence. The Holy of Holies of the temple represents the inner-core of the human being—the conscience; the place where God desires to dwell in the hearts and minds of mankind. In Psalm 91:1, it reads *"He who dwells in the secret place of the Most High shall abide under the shadow of the Almighty."* As long as the saint envelopes himself in Christ, the true tabernacle, there is the assurance given to him of abiding under God's shadow; that individual has God as his tent and covering.

The Feast of Tabernacles not only portrays God tabernacling with mankind by way of the incarnation but also further reveals His being with us in flesh through the power of God's Holy Spirit. Christ chose the temple because He wanted to be close to His people. However, in the New Testament the tabernacle/temple is the Saints who make up the church. In Ephesians 2:19-22 Paul speaks of the household of God as the body that has its foundation in Christ, the apostles and prophets. This building grows into a holy temple in the Lord . . . for a dwelling place of God through the Spirit.

"The word *temple* is not the Temple with all its porches and surrounding buildings but the inner sanctuary—the holy of holies. Today God does not dwell in a physical structure but in a spiritual body called the church . . .

Collectively, God dwells in each believer by the Holy Spirit, forming us into His Temple."[157]

Samuele Bacchiocchi mentioned the festival also "reveals the nature and mission of Christ"[158]—to make His home with mankind. John explains that Christ, the Word, "who was God in the beginning (1:1) manifested Himself in this world in a most tangible way, by pitching His tent"[159] in the midst of sinful flesh (v14). Christ, dwelling in human flesh, shows how humanity ought to see the body as the temple of the living God. Levy again notes that

> "The Tabernacle also prefigures individual Christians. Paul said, "Know ye not that your body is the temple [sanctuary] of the Holy Spirit who is in you, whom ye have of God, and ye are not your own?"(1 Cor. 6:19). As a sanctuary where the Spirit of God dwells, believers are not at liberty to allow their bodies to be used outside of His designed purposes for them."[160]

Consider what was said about the body in Songs of Solomon. It depicts the glory of God. Jesus Christ, in flesh, was tempted like we are, yet without sin; and humanity are to present their bodies as living sacrifices (Romans 12:1), holy and acceptable to God. In 1 Corinthians 6:19; 3:16

---

[157] Ibid

[158] Bacchiocchi, Samuele. 1996. God's Festivals in Scripture and History. Part 2 The Fall Festivals. Biblical Perspectives. Berrien Springs, Michigan 47

[159] ibid 47

[160] Levy, D. M. 1993. The Tabernacle: Shadows of the Messiah: Its sacrifices, services, and priesthood. Friends of Israel Gospel Ministry: Bellmawr, NJ

and 2 Corinthians 6:16; Paul admonishes believers to keep the temple of God (body) holy so He might dwell with them here on earth through His Holy Spirit.

The Feast of Tabernacles serves not only to reveal the nature and mission of Christ, but also to depict the glorious destiny of humanity. "In Revelation 7:9-17 and 21:1 to 22:5, the major themes are effectively used to portray the final ingathering of God's people in their harvest home."[161] The ultimate fulfilment of tabernacles will be on the earth when the saints are gathered in the presence of the Almighty. There will be no need for a temple as Revelation 21:22 points out, *"for the Lord Almighty and the Lamb are its temple;"* the tabernacle of God will be with men. In John 7:37-39, it shows that on the last and great day of the feast (eighth day) Christ stood up and called for those who thirst to come to him and drink of the living water. Christ was trumpeting the call to righteousness as He did with the woman at the well in John 4:1-26. Salvation will come alive to all mankind, Jew and Gentile, as depicted by this feast, which shows Jesus Christ as the true tabernacle.

The Feast of Tabernacles was celebrated with both the material and spiritual blessings of the harvest during the exodus experience and serves 'to foreshadow the blessings of the messianic age when "there shall be neither cold nor frost . . . continuous day . . . living water, and . . . security (Zech 14:6-7, 11)."[162] The feast shows that as Christ

---

161 Bacchiocchi, Samuele. 1996. God's Festivals in Scripture and History. Part 2 The Fall Festivals. Biblical Perspectives. Berrien Springs, Michigan 47

162 Bacchiocchi, Samuele. 1996. God's Festivals in Scripture and History. Part 2 The Fall Festivals. Biblical Perspectives.

tabernacled in the flesh (John 1:14), doing the command and will (John 4: 34) of the Father so were the first man and all humanity meant to do the commands of Yahweh. Jesus Christ did not incorporate evil as Adam did in His tent. First Peter 2:22 reads . . . *who did no sin, neither was guile found in his mouth.* It is because of sin that mankind is given an allotted time of six thousand years to repent and believe the Gospel. Repent of evil and believe God; that God loved us as Himself and willingly gave up His son Jesus Christ, to save mankind. If we take the scenario of a day equalling one thousand years it shows that mankind has been given six days or six thousand years to work at being good and obedient to the Father. After that, it will be God's turn. Saving mankind means rescuing him from death, but man will have to die in regards to the flesh.

For one week of the year (Leviticus 23: 33-36) the saints are commanded to tabernacle before God Almighty. The saints are required to leave the security of their homes and dwell in tents or booths. This is "beautifully typified in the ministry of Jesus the Messiah, who left His throne in heaven and tabernacled in human flesh (Jn. 1:14). In Christ we have a high priest, a perfect blood sacrifice, and access to God for all who put their trust in Him."[163] When the saints assemble in this way, it is a recognition and acknowledgement that Yahweh is the one who truly protects and watches over them with his banner of love. The saints live in the shadow (Psalm 91:1; Colossians 2:16) as God lovingly shelters them from the powerful, yet temporary rays of the enemy. Some

Berrien Springs, Michigan 46

[163] Levy, D. M. 1993. The Tabernacle: Shadows of the Messiah: Its sacrifices, services, and priesthood. Friends of Israel Gospel Ministry: Bellmawr, NJ

question why the departing of 'permanent' homes to dwell in temporary settings for a week. Again, take into account that the physical body, as home of the soul, was not meant to be permanent and sin caused the banishment of mankind from the presence of God and the Garden of Eden—his first physical home. In Revelation 21:1 we see that the earth (home) will be restored at the coming of Jesus Christ. First Corinthians 15:35-58 speaks of the glorious body that the saints will receive in order to inherit the Kingdom of God. We have inherited a temporary, corrupt body that if sown in love and obedience to the command of God will be raised incorruptible at the coming of our Lord and Saviour, Jesus Christ. Our temporary relocation for seven days is a type and shadow of the real thing to come.

The Feast of Tabernacles also tells us about the millennial reign of Christ when He shall appear in all his glory to save humanity by giving all the opportunity to become His children and heirs. First Timothy 2:3-6 and 2 Peter 3:8-9, show the desire of Yahweh, that all humanity be saved. Salvation is offered to all (Acts 2:21; John 3:16) and will be made possible by the wonderful Last Great Day of the Feast. Christ will return along with his saints to the earth to set up his Kingdom (Revelation 20:6; 5:10; Daniel 7:13-14; 26-27) binding Satan for a thousand years (Revelation 20:1-3) so that he cannot deceive the nations anymore. It is at this time that the opportunity will be given to all to be saved (Isaiah 2:3; 11:6-9; Zechariah 8:22-23; 14). Revelation 20 gives us a clear view of what will happen. In verses 7-11 it notes that after the thousand years are finished, Satan will again be set free to deceive those who will be exposed fully to the truth of Yahweh during the millennium. Some will be deceived and follow him and will be destroyed forever. In the verses following we see a resurrection of the dead standing before Yahweh to be judged from the books with the Book of Life being opened, at the Great White Throne Judgement. The parables of the 'Pearl of Great Price' and the 'Dragnet' found in Matthew 13: 45-46 and 47-50 respectively show what will happen on this Last Great Day. The pearl of great price is the church and the dragnet pictures the millennium. It is church that will work with Christ to bring in all those who will be called. The fate of those who reject the ways of Yahweh is addressed in verses 13-15, their names were not written in the Book of Life. The God of love is also a God who hates disobedience and will destroy all who fail to be obedient to Him. This feast is depicted by humanity keeping the miniature weekly Sabbath that ultimately teaches us about the joy and rest that can be found in the tabernacle.

The Reward for Obedience

Understanding the Gift of Immortality

Satan, in deceiving mankind into believing that he will not surely die, opened the door for the widespread belief that mankind has an immortal soul. This is not the only reason, the very fact that God chose to make man in his own image and likeness (Genesis 1:26) has led men to want to identify with the Creator on a far more spiritual level than he is at present. Some have also largely used the opportunity of the immortal soul doctrine to teach that heaven is the reward of the saved.

Let the scriptures and God's Holy Spirit be the guide toward the truth that is being sought. Remember that the issue of Sin and the Law is still being examined as the aim is to show that by the Law, immortality is the destiny of mankind, but we lost out on it at the beginning. It is the glory of God that mankind fell short of (Romans 3:23). Sin can also, be defined as mortality and if sin is mortality, then man does not have an immortal soul. Ezekiel 18:4 and 20 dogmatically disprove such disparity. If man already possesses immortality then there is no reward for those who are being saved because they already possess that which is promised—Eternal life.

Let us again start at the very beginning. Already mentioned is Genesis 1:26 where God made man in His own image and likeness; a prefiguring of what the incarnate Jesus Christ would look like in the flesh. Not that man has an immortal soul as is being professed by some. Now, in Genesis 2:7 it shows that man was dead before the breath of life was given to him, declaring him a living soul. It reads, *"and the Lord God formed man of the dust of the ground, and breathed into his nostrils the breath of life; and man became a living being."* Notice that it is the breath of life (spirit, wind) from the *One* who has life within himself (John 5:26) that made man a living soul—a living being. Man was basically dead, unconscious before the fact. He was not given a soul but became a living soul. Job 34:14-15 says if God should take back his spirit to himself, and gather to himself his breath, all flesh would perish together and man would return to dust. This enlightens us to the fact that man is both physical and spiritual and both aspects of him cease to exist at death. The question that is then being asked is—If man is in the image and likeness of God and God is immortal, then isn't it only logical for one to ascribe immortality to man's soul? Well, not quite! Observe that man came into existence at a point in time when he was formed from the dust of the ground; he did not always exist as Christ did from the beginning (John 1:1; 1 John 1:1; Revelation 19:13). Therefore, to ascribe immortality to the soul of man is not only a case of misinterpretation but is also an imposition.

Man is a soul making him a living, breathing creature like the animals but not possessing divinity (immortality). The reference to soul in the scriptures in both the Hebrew (*nephesh*) and Greek (*psyche*) equivalent literally means 'breath' and is used in reference to both animals and humans alike who are alive (Genesis 1:20, 21, 24; 2:19; 9:10, 12:15; Revelation 8:9; 16:3 etc.) or dead (Leviticus 21:1, 11; Numbers 6:6, 11; Matthew 10:28 etc.). However, humanity has an appearance of God—being made after the God-kind, unlike the animals, which were made 'after their kind.' "Soul" in the Bible nearly always refers to the fleshly nature, it is the only power a man has for expressing his true spirit."[164] This spirit imparts 'Godlike' qualities of mind such as, dominion, intelligence and reasoning ability but at death, returns to God who gave it (Ecclesiastes 12:7). The fact that this spirit enables consciousness in humans and returns to God after death does not allow for the assigning of immortality to the man. "Humans return to the dust (Genesis 3:19) whence they came, while the life-breath given by God returns to its original possessor. This is a picture of dissolution, not of immortality."[165] Man is a soul that can die as was declared by the Eternal, *'the soul that sinneth it shall die'* (Ezekiel 18:4, 20) and all have sinned (Romans 3:23). Romans 5:14 notes that death came through Adam and immortality and life came through Jesus Christ (2 Timothy 1:10). If death came to all through Adam and mankind has inherited his nature then the soul without the (spirit of God) is dead, only to be awakened by the call of the life giving Spirit of God.

164　Chambers, O. 1996, c1960. The philosophy of Sin: And other studies on the problem of man's moral life. Marshall, Morgan & Scott: Hants UK

165　Murphy, R. 2002. Vol. 23A: Word Biblical Commentary: Ecclesiastes. Word Biblical Commentary. Word, Incorporated: Dallas

If one should take a closer look at the teachings of some, it will be obvious that man's search for meaning leads him to question the state of his soul after death. In the temptation and sin of Adam and Eve (Genesis 3) death was the issue. Satan deliberately said, "*you will not die*" (v. 4) nullifying the authority and truth of the word of God. Adam and Eve did die to truth and the good that existed and became alive to evil, which is death. Obviously Satan's intention was to discredit the reputation of the Almighty by being a false witness against his neighbour (Exodus 20:16) in this matter of life after death. Always keep in mind the ultimate destiny of mankind—that of becoming 'God' through the process of character reproduction (freewill) and it was highlighted that this can only be done through spirit. Character reproduction is not an instantaneous thing but takes place over time through experiences or tests that require obedience. God's character is self-determined by His own free will (demonstrated in the life of Jesus Christ) and thus, in creating man in his own image and likeness, has given the same opportunity of choice to man. Mankind must be free to make his own decisions and, as a result, the superiority in appearance of man is in relation to God—the 'image and likeness' to which he was created. Man is a 'god' (Psalm. 82:6; John 10:34) but not 'The Immortal God' (1 Timothy 1:17, 6:16).

In the temptation and sin of humanity, God commanded Adam not to eat of the tree of the knowledge of good and evil and further stated why. "*For in the day that you eat of it you shall surely die*" (Genesis 2:17) but the spirit of evil, conjure otherwise (Genesis 3:4-5). In addressing the immortal issue, the symbolism of the trees cannot be ignored. Go back to what they signify. The Spirit of good, is the tree of life which is the love of God, and the spirit of evil is symbolized by the tree of the knowledge of good and evil (Genesis 2:9) which is the evil nature of the enemy. Let's clarify something about this tree of the 'knowledge of good and evil'—though mankind have a conscious knowledge of good he chooses evil over good almost always (Genesis 6:5; Romans 1:28-32). It is the knowledge of evil that kills. Earlier, it was stated that God's character is self-determined by His own free will. That is, God has knowledge of both good and evil. However, He chooses to do 'good'. That is His character and His created beings (mankind) have no less an opportunity if they are to be like him in character. One's choice determines one's character. Satan, though with the knowledge of good chose to do evil and so does humanity since Adam. Mankind is the spiritual property of Satan that God is buying back through the process of adoption.

Man was always a thinking being—he reasoned with his creator in the Garden of Eden. Therefore, the spirit in man has to do with his conscience—his mind and intellect. The word conscience means 'to be with knowledge' which supports Genesis 3:22 in saying, man has become like one of Us—he has knowledge of good and evil and knows when he is breaking the law. Man's conscience came to realize evil and, therefore, man is accountable for his actions based on knowledge and freewill. His conscience showed his shame when he tried to cover himself. Adam and Eve thought about their decision long and hard before following through to eat of the fruit. The physical eating of the fruit was the fulfilment of what they had conceived within the consciousness of their minds; thus making their death both physical and spiritual. They were tempted by their own desire . . . enticed by it . . . which finally gave birth to sin and death (James 1: 13-15). A thought that is said to be sinful does not really mature until one actually indulges in the act as mere temptation is not sin.

> "Our Lord had a body, and we read that He hungered; it was not a sin for Him to be hungry, but it would have been a sin for Him to have eaten during the forty days in the wilderness, because His Father's word at that time was that He should not eat." [166]

Not negating the words of Jesus Christ in Matthew 5:27-28 that a man looking at a woman to lust has committed adultery in his heart. Thus, to look deliberately at a woman lustfully, i.e., desiring or imagining a sexual relationship with her, is to commit adultery in one's heart. This is to violate the deepest intention of the law as now revealed by Jesus—the spiritual intent. In commenting Donald Hagner notes that

> "The idea of sinning in the heart through one's desires is already contained in the ten commandments, where one is forbidden to covet, among other things, the wife of a neighbor (Exod 20:17; Deut 5:21)."[167]

A man can look at a woman without allowing his mind to lust. It is allowing our minds to be enticed by what is seen that causes sin, hence the admonition "*be transformed*

---

[166] Chambers, O. 1996, c1960. The philosophy of Sin: And other studies on the problem of man's moral life. Marshall, Morgan & Scott: Hants UK

[167] Hagner, D. A. 2002. Vol. 33A: Word Biblical Commentary: Matthew 1-13. Word Biblical Commentary. Word, Incorporated: Dallas.

by the renewing of your mind, that you may prove what is that good and acceptable and perfect will of God" (Romans 12:2). The writer in Hebrews 4:15 tells us that Christ, our High Priest, was tempted in all points as we are yet without sin. Sin originates in the mind—the consciousness of man. It is both the conscious mind and the physical that dies.

It is a known fact that at death the physical body returns to the dust from which it came (Genesis 3:19). However, man's concern is, how can the soul die if the spirit that ignites it is from the Eternal Creator? Keep in mind that the flesh is useless without the consciousness of the mind/spirit/breath of God that gives life to lifeless beings. Just as the body could not/was unable to operate before the breath of God was given to it, so does it after death; there is no functioning (Ecclesiastes 12:7). As it was in the beginning so shall it be in the end. Before the physical aspect of man, he was a concept or thought of the Eternal God but needed a body to complete its existence. This was what God did at creation: He made a body so that man could exist.

A man dies when the spirit leaves the body and goes back to God. When this happens the soul ceases to exist because it cannot function without a body. It lies dormant, dead and unconscious. The Word of God affirms that the soul can die—the word of God is the scriptural evidence. In Matthew 10:28, Jesus taught that the soul can be destroyed. It says, *"And do not fear those who can kill the body but cannot kill the soul. But rather fear Him who is able to destroy both soul and body in hell."* God the Father is the person with the authority to awaken a soul to life eternal or to damn it to eternal hell. When the man Jesus Christ died, it was God the Father who raised Him from death to life immortal (Acts

3:15; 13:30; Romans 10:9; Galatians 1:1; Ephesians 1:20; 1Peter 1:21); so it will be with mankind at the sound of the last trumpet. The trumpet call to life everlasting will sound and the dead in Christ shall rise first (1 Thessalonians. 4:16). The man who dies and has set His conscience free by doing the will (obeying the law) of the Father will be raised like Christ did (Romans 2:7). He will be raised incorruptible (1 Corinthians 15:52); with a different body from the one that was subject to sin and decay (1 Corinthians 15:35-38). It is at the resurrection that man will become immortal.

The Bible compares death to sleep or taking a rest: it is a state of being unconscious and unaware of what is happening in the surroundings. Jesus, in John 11, spoke of sleep as it relates to the death of Lazarus, mentioning that it was for the glory of God. In verses 25-26 of John 11, Jesus said to Martha *"I am the resurrection and the life. He who believes in Me, though he may die, He shall live."* When the dead in Christ are raised up it will be as if they had not die—they rise to do the continuous will of the Father and the Son. Beasley-Murray in commenting notes that, "It signifies not so much a rejection of Martha's faith as an extension of it and a setting of it on a sure foundation. The eschatological rule of God for which Martha hopes, with all its blessings for humankind, is vested in Jesus."[168] In Ephesians 2:1-5, Paul spoke of the saints who were dead being made alive through the love of Christ. All consciousness of man at present is dead. However, Mankind awakening by the call of God is in relation to His destiny

---

[168] Beasley-Murray, G. R. 2002. Vol. 36: Word Biblical Commentary: John. Word Biblical Commentary. Word, Incorporated: Dallas

as God-beings, the truth to which God in Christ Jesus proclaimed. It is the soul that died and will be awakened to be clothed with immortality at the coming Kingdom of God; the soul that lives in obedience to the righteousness of God. Look at 1 Corinthians 15, where Paul illustrates the resurrection from the dead. If Christ was not raised from the dead neither will mankind. In verse 53, he noted that this mortal must put on immortality'. If this is so, then immortality is not something that mankind possesses now or will gain immediately after death. He has an inclination based on the fact that God has placed eternity (Ecclesiastes 3:11) in his heart as his destiny but he has no immortality.

Scripture tells us that Satan as a spirit being will cease to exist so will the soul who disobeys God. Psalm 139:11, 12 shows that darkness cannot hide from light. Evil cannot hide from good and that's the reason why David could end His prayer with a request to be cleansed from evil. He said in verse 23-24 *"search me, O God, and know my heart: Try me, and know my thoughts; And see if there be any wicked way in me, and lead me in the way everlasting."* David, a man after God's own heart was asserting not so much his hatred of the people but that of the evil that God wants to rid us of.

Adam died because of sin and, therefore, it required a second Adam to make atonement for the sins of humanity. For as in Adam all died, so in Christ all will be made alive (1 Corinthians 15:22). Christ made us alive by purifying our conscience from dead works to serve the true and living God. Jesus Christ had to die as the righteous Adam to save man. Jesus in witnessing to Nicodemus in John 3:1-21 told him that he must be born again to enter the Kingdom of God.

Jesus emphasized that he be born of the water and Spirit. Remember it was the Spirit of God that made man alive but he chose to ignore God's command at the beginning and obeyed the spirit of evil. Beasley-Murray notes that to be begotten "of water and Spirit" therefore means rebirth of spiritual seed, as in 1 John 3:9."[169] This spiritual rebirth is the awakening of the spirit of mankind that needs to be born again with the spirit of 'good' that leads to righteousness and life. Second Corinthians 5:17; Ephesians 4:24 speak of the new creature created in righteousness and holiness in Christ Jesus. It is the spirit of our minds that condemn us to death that is presently being transformed in newness with the Spirit of God. Paul's admonition in Romans 12:2 states *"And do not conform to this world, but be transformed by the renewing of your mind, that you may prove what is that good and acceptable and perfect will of God."* In the book of **Romans** the author notes that world or age is in accordance to the Jewish view; the present evil age and the blessed age to come. He notes then that "transformation by the renewal of the mind, then, involves the penetration of the coming age into the present evil age, believers resist the pressures to conform to the present evil age by the renewal of their minds . . . to understand the truth."[170]

All of humanity lost out on this great gift of salvation—immortality; therefore, all are spiritually dead due to Adam's disobedience. Every single human being is held captive by the power of death until awakened by the

[169] Beasley-Murray, G. R. 2002. Vol. 36: Word Biblical Commentary: John. Word Biblical Commentary. Word, Incorporated: Dallas

[170] Schreiner. Thomas. R. 1998. Romans. Baker Book House. Grand Rapids, Michigan. 647

spirit of God. However, all souls will be given a chance to accept or reject this precious gift of salvation (some now; others at the millennium). All are unconscious to what sin and the law is until awakened by the call of God's Holy Spirit. For the record, this death is both a physical and spiritual one—death of the conscience that cannot again be renewed to life; once it has been formed and lived out. However, this state is for those to whom the truth of God has been presently revealed through the call (Hebrews 6:4-6). If one continues in rebellion of sin until the conscience is seared with a hot iron, that soul will be severed from God and like Satan's cannot be renewed by truth to life eternal. William Lane points out

> "What is signified is not simply instruction for salvation but the renewal of the mind and of life . . . If those who have enjoyed a full and authentic Christian experience should then fall away, a renewal to repentance is impossible (v 6) . . . to repudiate Christ is to embrace the "impossible." [171]

The soul that rejects the truth will be tormented in hell like the rich man in Luke 16:19-31 who killed his conscience by not doing good to his neighbour who, at death, was consoled in the bosom of Abraham. The bosom of Abraham signifies the close relationship Abraham had with Father, the seed through whose earthly loin Jesus descended. It is man that God will judge and those who have lived faithfully, in love and faith, will be renewed in

---

[171]   Lane, W. L. 2002. Vol. 47A: Word Biblical Commentary: Hebrews 1-8. Word Biblical Commentary. Word, Incorporated: Dallas

spirit (Revelation 20:4). Those not renewed will be thrown in the lake of fire to be consumed. This is not a continuous burning hell but that which is burnt and blown away. If man has already possessed immortality (eternal life), what is the use of the promise of redemption? What is mankind being saved from? Isn't it from death to life—life eternal?

Conclusion

In summary, the law that Adam and Eve broke was not the Ten Commandments in a literal sense but the eternal covenant that makes mankind one with the Eternal God of the universe. Sin is through the law, (Romans 7:7) it is the act of coveting. This evil force is seen in our actions and decisions operating on and within us. Romans 5:14 shows that Adam's sin typifies and stamps its character on everyone since time began; there is no getting around it. Mankind's redemption journey in achieving the purpose for which he was created was fulfilled in the person of Jesus Christ who came not to annul the Law but to fulfil it. The law was added in the form of the Ten Commandments because of the transgression of the command to love the Lord God with all thine heart and with all thy soul. There was nothing moral or immoral about the command of the Eternal. God was simply giving mankind the option of being fully in His image and likeness—true 'sonship' privileges. This is such a mind-boggling truth that for some it seems hardly true and, thus, warrants philosophical and intellectual debate. All of which value nothing, if their conclusion does not equal what Yahweh has revealed in His Word. God chose to reveal His solution to mankind's redemption through the person of Jesus Christ. The love of God is expressly seen in the person of Jesus Christ who kept the law perfectly by being the Passover Lamb, the Unleavened Bread which came down from heaven; the first fruit of man's righteousness given through the Holy Spirit of God. This He did by trumpeting the call to a righteous life by His atoning sacrifice while tabernacling in human flesh. There is no other way to know who God is except through the person of Jesus Christ. In John 14:6, Jesus said to him; *"I am the way, the truth, and the life. No one comes to the Father except through Me."* Those who claim to know who God is without acknowledging who Christ is, are anti-Christ (1 John 2:22); they have no claim. They have no authority to do so because such power is given by Christ to those called in obedience and sanctification of the truth (John 17:17-19).

There are some who ignore and question the present day observance of the seventh day Sabbath and Feast Days of God not realizing they are questioning God's relevance in our lives and our need to obey Him. The claim that they are no longer binding on Christians today shows mankind rebellion against the divine. They cite texts such as, Colossians 2:16—'So let no one judge you in food or in drink, or regarding a festival or a new moon or Sabbaths.' However, they have negated v. 17 that says . . . *"which are a shadow of things to come, but the substance is of Christ."* Christ is the substance of the Sabbath and Feast Days and those who practice them worship and celebrate the Eternal God because it was through these days that the Father chose to reveal himself to humanity. Some, in their quest to do away with the commands of God, has not taken into consideration the word which begins verse 17—*so,* which means as a result of, or consequently. Paul was not addressing the discarding away of the feast days or Sabbaths. He said let no one judge you. No one can pass judgement if there is not something to judge. The saints were keeping the feasts of God but there were those (Gnostics) who felt that righteousness should take the form of punishing the body because the body was sinful. There is no passage of scripture that gives authority to the abandonment of the feasts days and Sabbaths of God. In fact in Ezekiel 20:12, God stated that He gave the Sabbaths (Feasts days) as a sign and that the people may come to know that He was the God who sanctifies. It reads, *"Moreover I also gave them My Sabbaths, to be a sign between them and Me, that they might know that I am the Lord who sanctifies them"*. God is the sign of the Feast Days which is portrayed for unbelievers, not believers, and the entire world stand in unbelief. Paul notes in 1 Timothy 6:11 that even the justified need to pursue righteousness which indisputably involves the commands of Yahweh and the keeping of the Feast Days. How will the saints know the God who sanctifies if they neglect the sanctification of God through Christ in the shadow of the Sabbath and Feasts Days? It is definitely not by observing Sunday, Easter or Christmas or any other time forbidden by Yahweh.

If mankind chooses not to worship God on His terms they cannot claim to be worshiping God in Spirit and truth (John 4:23). Therefore, their awaiting the eternal redemption is in vain and God will say depart from me, I know you not. God chose to reveal His immortal gift to humanity through His Son Jesus Christ (1Timothy 1:17) in whom we are told to believe. The ball is now in the court of the individual to choose life over death—immortal life (the hope and destiny of the beloved) over eternal death.

References

Achtemeier, P. J., Harper & Row, P., & Society of Biblical Literature. 1985. *Harper's Bible Dictionary*. Includes index. (1st ed.). Harper & Row: San Francisco

Aune, D. E. 2002. *Vol. 52B*: *Word Biblical Commentary: Revelation 6-16*. Word Biblical Commentary. Word, Incorporated: Dallas

Bacchiocchi, Samuele. (1995). *God's Festivals in Scripture and History: Part 1 The Spring Festivals.* Biblical Perspectives. Berrien Springs, Michigan.

Bacchiocchi, Samuele. 1996. *God's Festivals in Scripture and History. Part 2 The Fall Festivals.* Biblical Perspectives. Berrien Springs, Michigan

Bahnsen. Greg L., Walter C. Kaiser Jr., Douglas J. Moo., Wayne G. Strickland., Willem A. VanGemeren (1996) *Five Views on Law and Gospel.* Zondervan Publishing House. Grand Rapids, Michigan.

Beasley-Murray, G. R. 2002. *Vol. 36*: *Word Biblical Commentary: John*. Word Biblical Commentary. Word, Incorporated: Dallas

Chambers, O. 1996, c1960. *The Philosophy of Sin : And other studies on the problem of man's moral life.* Marshall, Morgan & Scott: Hants UK

Davidson, R. M. A. 2001, c 1986. *Ecclesiastes and the Song of Solomon.* The Daily Study Series. Westminster John Knox Press: Louisville.

Dunn, J. D. G. 2002. *Vol. 38A: Word Biblical Commentary: Romans 1-8.* Word Biblical Commentary. Word, Incorporated: Dallas

Dunn, J. D. G. 2002. *Vol. 38B: Word Biblical Commentary: Romans 9-16.* Word Biblical Commentary. Word, Incorporated: Dallas

Durham, J. I. 2002. *Vol. 3: Word Biblical Commentary: Exodus.* Word Biblical Commentary. Word, Incorporated: Dallas

Easton, M. 1996, c1897. *Easton's Bible Dictionary.* Logos Research Systems, Inc.: Oak Harbor, WA

Edwards, Wesley P: (2008) *Understanding Reason and Faith.* Editor@FreethoughtDebator.com

Hagner, D. A. 2002. *Vol. 33A: Word Biblical Commentary: Matthew 1-13.* Word Biblical Commentary. Word, Incorporated: Dallas

Hagner, D. A. 2002. *Vol. 33B: Word Biblical Commentary: Matthew 14-28.* Word Biblical Commentary. Word, Incorporated: Dallas

Hayford, J. W., & Curtis, G. 1997, c1994. *Pathways to Pure Power: Learning the depth of love's power, a study of first Corinthians*. C1994 by Jack W. Hayford. Spirit-Filled Life Bible Discovery Guides. Thomas Nelson: Nashville

Hayford, J. W., & Hagen, K. A. 1997, c1996. *Redemption and Restoration: Reversing life's greatest losses, a study of Ruth and Esther*. C1996 by Jack W. Hayford. Spirit-Filled Life Bible Discovery Guides. Thomas Nelson: Nashville

Hodge, C. 2000. *An Exposition of First Corinthians* (electroniced.). Ephesians Four Group: Escondito, California

http://www.scribd.com/doc/8616689/A-Study-on-His-Return-on-a-Jewish-Festival

Lane, W. L. 2002. *Vol. 47A: Word Biblical Commentary: Hebrews 1-8*. Word Biblical Commentary. Word, Incorporated: Dallas

Lane, W. L. 2002. *Vol. 47B: Word Biblical Commentary: Hebrews 9-13*. Word Biblical Commentary. Word, Incorporated: Dallas

Levy, D. M. 1993. *The tabernacle : Shadows of the Messiah: Its sacrifices, services, and priesthood*. Friends of Israel Gospel Ministry: Bellmawr, NJ

MacArthur, J. J. 1997, c1997. *The MacArthur Study Bible* (electroniced.). Word Pub.: Nashville

Martin. R. P. 2002. *Vol. 48: Word Biblical Commentary: James.* Word Biblical Commentary. Word, Incorporated: Dallas.

Martin. R. P. 2004. *Vol. 43: Word Biblical Commentary: Philippians.* Word Biblical Commentary. Word, Incorporated: Dallas.

McGee, J. V. 2001, c1988. *Ruth and Esther: Women of faith* (electronic ed.). Thomas Nelson Publishers: Nashville

McGee, J. V. 2001, c1995. *Love, Liberation & the Law: The Ten Commandments* (electroniced.). Thomas Nelson Publishers: Nashville 51.

McQuaid, E. 1986. *The Outpouring: Jesus in the Feasts of Israel.* Moody Press: Chicago

Moller, F. P. 1998, c1997. *Vol. 3: From Sin to Salvation.* Words of light and life. Van Schaik Religious Books: Pretoria

Murphy, R. 2002. *Vol. 23A: Word Biblical Commentary: Ecclesiastes.* Word Biblical Commentary. Word, Incorporated: Dallas

New Catholic Encyclopedia (2003) Volume 6, page 678

Pink, A. W. 1999. *The Law and the Saint.* Logos Research Systems, Inc.: Oak Harbor, WA

Pink, A. W. 2000. *The Ten Commandments* (electroniced.). Ephesians Four Group: Escondido, CA

Rugh, W. 1998. *Christ in the Tabernacle: Person and work of Jesus Christ*. Woodlawn Electronic Publishing: Willow Grove, PA

Ryken, L., Wilhoit, J., Longman, T., Duriez, C., Penney, D., & Reid, D. G. 2000, c1998. *Dictionary of Biblical Imagery* (electronic ed.). InterVarsity Press: Downers Grove, IL

Schreiner. Thomas R. (2003) *Romans*. Baker Book House. Grand Rapids, Michigan.

Schreiner. Thomas R. (2003). *Romans*. Baker Book House. Grand Rapids, Michigan.

Scott, B. 1997. *The Feasts of Israel* (electroniced.). The Friends of Israel Gospel Ministry, Inc.: Bellmawr, New Jersey

Smalley, S. S. 2002. *Vol. 51*: *Word Biblical Commentary: 1,2,3 John*. Word Biblical Commentary. Word, Incorporated: Dallas

Walker, Williston, Richard A. Norris, David W. Lotz, Robert T. Handy. (1985) *A History of the Christian Church*. 4th Ed. Simon and Schuster Inc. New York

Watson, Thomas. 2000. *The Ten Commandments* (electroniced.). Ephesians Four Group: Escondito, California

Wenham, G. J. 2002. *Vol. 1: Word Biblical Commentary: Genesis 1-15*. Word Biblical Commentary. Word, Incorporated: Dallas

Wenham, G. J. 2002. *Vol. 1: Word Biblical Commentary: Genesis 1-15*. Word Biblical Commentary. Word, Incorporated: Dallas

Wood, D. R. W., Wood, D. R. W., & Marshall, I. H. 1996, c1982, c1962. *New Bible Dictionary*. Includes index. (electroniced. of 3rd ed.). InterVarsity Press: Downers Grove. 775

www.http://biblicalholidays.com

www.torah.org. Avraham Avinu and the War to free the Minds of Humanity. HaRav Ariel Bar Tzadok (2009)

www.torah.org.HaRav Ariel Bar Tzadok. 2008 Secrets of Shabat Observance.

www.torah.org

About the Author

Oddeth Samantha Burton was born in St. Catherine Jamaica, an ardent lover of Bible doctrines. This love prompted her to explore the issue of sin and the law in a bid to share it with others.

Presently a Master of Arts student at the University of the West Indies, Mona studying Media and Mass Communication in a attempt to communicate the Message of the Gospel in a simple, more profound manner. She also holds a Bachelor of Arts Degree in Theology and Counselling from the Jamaica Theological Seminary.

Miss Burton is a member of the Church of God International, Spanish Town, St. Catherine Jamaica. She actively participates in the writing of the Adult Sabbath School Quarterly, a study guide for its members. She has conducted numerous bible studies and written and submitted articles for the Canadian Prevail Magazine and the International News Magazine.